Jesus untouched by the Church

His Teachings in the Gospel of Thomas

Cover: Sixth century icon of Jesus from the monastery church of Saint Catherine, Mount Sinai.

BY THE SAME AUTHOR:

The Gospel of Thomas, a Presentation

Thirty Essays on the Gospel of Thomas

George Fox Speaks for Himself

Jesus untouched by the Church

His Teachings in the Gospel of Thomas

By Hugh McGregor Ross

Calligraphy by John Blamires

William Sessions Limited
York · England

Published 1998 by William Sessions Limited
The Ebor Press, York, YO3 9HS, England

Text, format, arrangement and presentation
Copyright © 1998 Hugh McGregor Ross

ISBN 1850722137

All rights reserved. No part of this book may be reproduced, stored in a retrieval system or transmitted, or used by an internet service provider, or utilized in any form or by any means, electronic or photographic, without permission in writing from the Publisher.

Calligraphy for cover and main text
by John Blamires, Brighouse, HD6 2BQ

Origination by Alpha Studios, Stroud, GL5 3JQ
Typeset in Baskerville font 11.5 point on 14

Printed and bound by The Ebor Press

The author may be reached at Didymos Thomas Books
Simmondley, Painswick, Glos. GL6 6XA, England

CONTENTS

SETTING THE SCENE

Escapes and Discoveries	page 3
The Thomas Text	6
The Thomas People	14
Literary Features	20
Relationship with the Bible	24

THE TEACHINGS

The Good News Brought by Thomas	31
The Summary	33
Discrimination	37
Seeing the Master	41
Turning to the Master	49
To Know and Metanoïa	51
Birth and Death	57
Light at the Centre	60
Finding the Light at the Centre	62
Quenching Ahamkāra	64
Oneness	79
Spiritual Life Essential	92
From Small Things Great Grow	94
The Way to the Kingdom	96
Spiritual Richness	104
Monakos and Courage	108
Images	111
Happiness	117
Old Order and New Way	123
Beyond Femininity	129
Wealth in Poverty	132
Austerity	133
Jesus' Disappointment	135
Wise Sayings	140
The Consummation	143
Acknowledgements	148
Index to Sayings	150

v

A disciple expresses his affection and gratitude to his revered Teacher

Setting the Scene

Escapes and Discoveries

ONLY ONE BOOK recording the Teachings of Jesus, and only a single ancient copy of that book, has escaped being touched by the Church. At no time have its contents been influenced by Churchmen, and it does not reflect the doctrines developed by the Christian Church. It is an original, independent.

The book comprises an unadorned collection of sayings by Jesus, recorded by his disciple Thomas, so that we may call it the Thomas Text. We know from ancient documents that after the crucifixion of Jesus in about 30 A.D. Thomas was assigned to take what he had been taught to the East, to Syria and India. There are very strong traditions in Southern India, amounting to a certainty, that he reached there in 52 A.D. The only viable scenario is that Thomas recorded these sayings before leaving for such a journey. This makes the Thomas Text earlier, perhaps by a whole generation, than any of the books or epistles accepted by the Church for inclusion in the New Testament.

We now also know that in those very early days a spiritual community grew up using the Thomas Text as their primary scripture. It extended from Egypt, through Palestine to Syria and beyond.

However, that community and especially the Thomas Text incurred the displeasure and ultimately the condemnation of the evolving Christian Church. Thus Bishop Hippolytus, head of the Church of Rome who died in 236 A.D., had effectively deterred any of his followers from using the Text, and in 367 Archbishop Athanasius of Alexandria sent out an edict against all heretical teachings and apocryphal books. This was almost certainly the occasion, and the cause, for monks of the monastery of St Palamon at Chenoboskia about 600 kilometres up the Nile to collect 52 books, in twelve volumes, from their library and hide them in a big earthenware jar beside a large rock below the cliffs that here border the river.

Thus hidden in the sand these treasures of their library escaped the Archbishop's investigators, escaped the demise and destruction of their monastery, escaped the ultimate extinction of the Thomas People in the seventh century, escaped the devastating invasion of Egypt by the Persians when books of the greatest Library in the world at Alexandria were thrown into the furnaces for the hypocaust of the building, escaped the attention of Churchmen in the centuries of the Inquisition and even their narrow mindedness that was so difficult for Darwin.

In 1945 this jar was discovered by some simple peasants. The volumes escaped a hair-raising series of mishaps[1] including fire, barter for paltry sums, being in the hands of a one-eyed bandit to avoid police, bargaining by unscrupulous dealers, being ignored by Western theologians, until they finally rested in Cairo, their contents and significance unknown.

However, by 1956 Professor Guilles Quispel of Holland had begun to study some of the volumes, whereupon he discovered that one book was significantly different from all the others and comprised this collection of sayings by Jesus. He, in fact, had to escape for his life from Egypt at the outbreak of the Suez Crisis, but carried with him photographs of the pages of the Thomas Text. With four other scholars he re-established the original text from the manuscript and first published it in English in 1959[2].

These sayings are almost all enigmatic and some are at first very difficult to understand. This is because they are dealing with spiritual Truth at a high level. They usually take the form of mini-parables, with an outer meaning and a deeper inner spiritual meaning. The first to make real progress in discovering these hidden inner meanings were the French scholars of the Association Métanoïa, publishing their works in 1975[3] and 1979[4].

Time is a major element in discovering the spiritual meanings. It is a reciprocal process—the sayings have an influence on the person studying them, and that increasing awareness permits a clearer recognition of what the sayings mean. A little thought will show that this awakening must have been the purpose in Jesus giving his sayings, and in Thomas recording them.

Having worked with these sayings for about twenty years, the present author carrying out a simple experiment discovered that by merely rearranging the sequence of the sayings in the original Thomas Text, by putting like with like, a coherent set of spiritual Teachings by Jesus is revealed.

So not only have these sayings of Jesus escaped in the sense of having avoided being touched by the Church and in the physical sense of avoiding many dangers, until they could be discovered in our more open-minded and enquiring age; but also their inner spiritual meanings have now escaped in the sense of being released, so they may be discovered by anyone who earnestly seeks these spiritual Teachings of Jesus.

1   'The Discovery of the Nag Hammadi Codices' by J M Robinson, The Biblical Archaeologist, vol 42, No 4, Autumn 1979

2   'The Gospel According to Thomas' by A Guillaumont, H-Ch Puech, G Quispel, W Till and Yassah 'Abd Al Masīḥ. Published 1959 and 1976 by E Brill, Leyden, Holland

3   'L'Évangile Selon Thomas' by Phillipe de Suarez. Published 1975 by Association Métanoïa, 26200, Montélimar, France

4   'Évangile Selon Thomas' by É Gillabert, P Bourgeois and Y Haas. Published 1979 by Association Métanoïa

The Thomas Text

THE THOMAS TEXT comprises a unique collection of 114 sayings of Jesus. It starts with the statement, probably by Thomas:

> *These are the hidden logia*
> *which the living Jesus spoke*
> *and Didymos Judas Thomas wrote.*

The word logia, or saying, is the plural of Greek logion.* This is related to Logos, which we translate as Word. However in Greek usage this has a very special meaning, approximating to the Divine. The greatest example is the Prologue to the Gospel of John "In the Beginning was the Word . . ." So a logion is a saying that has a connotation of the divine.

The living Jesus here means the person who lived and walked in the countries we now call Palestine, Israel and Jordan. It does not mean some abstract being revealed in a dream or vision.

Written almost certainly means dictated. In those days very few people could write—and it seems Jesus and Thomas were no exceptions. What a person did was to seek out a scribe from the market place, and dictate to him. This was the normal practice even for personal letters or business notes.

The birth name Judas clearly means one born a Jew. His other names are Greek, both meaning twin. They must have been given him, whether by Jesus or his fellow-disciples we cannot tell, as a recognition of a spiritual twin-ship to Jesus. He appears in his Text as one who really saw inwardly the nature and stature of Jesus, who had a special awareness of his quality. A tradition for this was still alive when Leonardo da Vinci painted his

---

* Usually pronounced with a soft g.

'Last Supper' in about 1500, for the figure at the right hand of Jesus, generally regarded as Thomas, is the only serene disciple, as though he understood what was happening. Even today icons of Thomas from the Orthodox Church of Russia express him with a spiritual sensitivity.

That spiritual twin-ship is of great relevance to the authenticity of the Thomas Text. It is well known that when a group of people hear a speaker, at a lecture or oration, they are apt to recall different interpretations of what was said. But one who has a good awareness of what was being said is likely to interpret and remember it the most correctly. It would provide a good foundation for the Thomas Text. Furthermore, in those days when literature was rare people tended to develop much better memories than ours. So what Thomas remembered could well have remained correctly until he dictated to the scribe.

That opening statement is immediately followed by:

He who finds the inner meaning of these logia
will find Life independent of death.

The first phrase links up with 'hidden' at the very beginning. The ancient word used for hidden is the same as that used in the saying about a treasure that had been buried which was found by a man diligently searching. So these logia are sayings with an outward form and yet also with a deep inner meaning within them. They are akin to small-scale parables, and Jesus is acknowledged as being unsurpassed in his use of those to convey his Teachings.

These are not secret or esoteric sayings, or only for the few. They are for anyone who wishes to seek and find the inner meanings that lie, merely hidden, within them. Such seeking involves work. That is inevitable, for the aim of Jesus is to raise us from our ordinary life to a higher level, in order that we might find the Life, in the here and now, that is independent of the death of the body.

Thereafter all the sayings in the Thomas Text are direct records of what Jesus said. They are almost all introduced by

THE THOMAS TEXT

"Jesus said". There is very little narrative, except for brief phrases to set the scene such as:

His disciples questioned, they said to him:
or *Jesus saw children who were being suckled.*
or *They showed Jesus a gold coin*

A striking feature of all these sayings is that they are of the Semitic style.* They are structured in short phrases, which complement one another, or make contrasts to heighten the impact, or form a hierarchical series leading to a greater significance. These short phrases are reflected in the Text, both in the ancient language and also when they are translated into a modern European language. This style of speaking and writing is entirely different from the Greek style, which we have inherited, for that forms long sentences with several topics, just like this one.

It is thus clear that Jesus' thought pattern was based on Aramaic, his mother tongue from childhood. Scholars have even found in the Thomas Text distinct Aramaisms,** usually just a few words. However, it becomes very clear from the ancient document that he sometimes used an Aramaic idiom and words and sometimes a Greek idiom and words. This reflects the fact that in his time and place about one in ten of the population were Jews, and the others of a culture called Hellenist. This was derived from Greek culture, which had spread all round the countries of the eastern Mediterranean. It was simpler and lacked the finesse of the great city states of Greece, but it had much the same practices—in politics, sport, ways of living—and especially copied much of the thought and concepts of classical Greece. The language used by the Hellenists was koine Greek, a somewhat simplified form.

---

* The main Semitic languages are Aramaic, Hebrew, Arabic and Syriac. At that time Aramaic was the common language used for trade and commerce in an enormous area from the Middle East to the whole of India. Greek was the other great common language, used in all countries of the eastern Mediterranean.

** 'Sémitismes dans les logia de Jésus retrouvés à Nag-Hammâdi' by A Guillaumont, Journal Asiatique, CCXLVI, 1958

The fact that we find in this ancient document Jesus using sometimes the Greek idiom, when he must have been speaking to Hellenists, and sometimes the Aramaic idiom, when speaking to Jews, is another significant clue to the authenticity of the Thomas Text. Otherwise, if it had been done over by some editor or redactor in antiquity, those distinctions would have been the first to be removed.

Scholars generally agree that the Thomas Text was originally written in Greek. This implies that when recording those sayings of Jesus spoken in Aramaic they must have been translated. One can suppose that Thomas, whose spiritual names were Greek, may have been well equipped to do this. However, he must have been very sensitive to the intended meanings, for he did not obscure distinctive Aramaic or Jewish concepts.

The copy we have of the Thomas Text is written primarily in Coptic. This is an Egyptian language nowadays rarely used, mainly in the liturgy of the Coptic Church of Egypt and Ethiopia. It was a language created or devised at the start of our era specifically to permit documents, specially of philosophical or spiritual types, written in Greek and then circulating round the eastern Mediterranean, to be made intelligible to Egyptians. It took one or two centuries to develop. It is significant that when a list is made of all the words used in the Thomas Text about 60 per cent of them are in Coptic and 40 per cent in Greek; furthermore, it is the simple words that are in Coptic, and Greek is used for the more complex. This implies that the Thomas Text may have been translated into Coptic fairly early in our era. Even so, it must have been done carefully, for the Semitic qualities, and the different Aramaic and Greek idioms, have come through to us. Naturally, all this throws a great responsibility on present-day translation into any European language.

Coptic is written with the Greek alphabet, together with six letters taken from a previous Egyptian alphabet Demotic (not hieroglyphic picture-symbols). Our ancient document is a copy of the Coptic translation, and we know it is a complete copy of what the copying monk had before him because he has filled out the last line with little symbols, like a lawyer sometimes does today. Scholars can see that the copier made some mistakes, typical of those anyone makes when copying by hand from one document to another, and can correct them. However, these errors are few, which may imply that what we have is a copy from the first Coptic translation, not a copy of a copy.

It is written with capital letters only, for the small letters that make writing quicker were invented only later. Also, it has neither spaces between words nor any punctuation, for they were also invented later. In fact, the whole document is just an unbroken string of letters. When the monk got to the end of a line he merely went on to the next, irrespective of whether a word ended there.

What all this amounts to is that a text in those days was a means of recording spoken words, the only one they had, in order that spoken words might be reproduced for others, by one of the few people who could read. To aid this, our ancient document uses two vocalization marks to indicate emphasis and structure, but it has none of the aids to reading we are accustomed to.

One of the aims of this present book is to provide a transition, to form a bridge, between that ancient spoken-only document and our present day practice of reading literature, and even reading it silently, and yet to convey the intended meanings.

At the finish of the ancient written Text itself, a little exclamation of praise has been added, from which come the usual titles the Gospel according to Thomas or the Gospel of Thomas. However, it is important to distinguish it from the gospels of the Bible. Outwardly there is the marked difference that it contains virtually no narrative or descriptive content about Jesus, whereas we have to rely on the gospels of the Bible for that.

But at a deeper level, the internal evidence of this ancient book, when properly appreciated, all points to its being a well-remembered and unadorned recording of sayings of Jesus. From this, many people may find it has a self-authenticating quality. It has not got woven into it the concepts and doctrines of the emerging Christian Church. Thus in a certain but important sense it may be regarded as pre-Christian.

The ancient document is written very clearly in black ink, which has not faded, on vegetable parchment. This was made —and still is made for craft purposes—from the pith of a reed that grows in Egypt. Strips of pith are opened out, laid side by side and flattened by rubbing until they glue themselves together and form a smooth writing material. It is a pale yellow colour.

In those days it was normal to make long strips of parchment which were used as scrolls, as in a modern Jewish synagogue. However, the books from that library at Chenoboskia were unusual in that the parchment was cut into double-pages, these were written on using both sides, then folded over and secured into a cover by a thong; just like our books.

The Thomas Text is one of many copied into a single volume. Its cover is tooled with attractive patterns. To make such a volume in those days was a considerable technical achievement.

The copy of the Thomas Text may easily have been one or two centuries old by the time it was buried, so some corners or edges of pages have gone. Also, over the centuries the parchment has become brittle, so there are a few small holes. No wonder after all the dangerous adventures it went through. However, scholars have reconstructed the writing over all those defects; fortunately none of the reconstructions affect the meaning of what is written.

Therefore what we have is a complete document from antiquity. This is a marked contrast to what Bible scholars usually have to work with, often only tiny scraps or quotations from which they try to draw out meaning or conclusions.

We may now turn to consider some general features of what is written in the Thomas Text. First, not only do these sayings have an outer and deeper inner meanings, but also Jesus, like other great spiritual teachers, uses symbolic language and imagery. Symbolic language works not just on the mind but essentially on the heart and the imagination. It has a power to reach levels within us that ordinary language fails to touch, it can convey an awareness in a way that plain words cannot do.

Furthermore, when the form and structure of the Thomas Text is considered as a whole, it becomes clear that it is not only reflecting a living form of speech, but also that it is very definitely not a studied literary composition. It has a distinctive vitality.

Secondly, let us return to the opening phrase:

These are the hidden sayings

The word 'hidden' can be taken at two levels. The first relates to each saying taken alone, where it is given as a mini-parable for which the hearer or reader has to do work to find the intended inner spiritual meaning. This kind of hiding is inherent in the nature of the sayings. The work involved is inherent in the teaching technique Jesus used. Very often it may involve throwing overboard some baggage carried inwardly—and in the case of the Teachings of the Thomas Text that may be other doctrines learnt in established Churches. A very apt analogy for the work is in climbing a mountain. At the summit there is the splendour of being able to look down in all directions on the country around. But the real satisfaction derives from the effort needed to make the ascent and overcome the difficulties. To go up by cable-car or rack-railway gives the same views, but lacks the inner satisfaction and worth.

At the second level when the sayings are considered as a whole it is the Teachings of Jesus that are hidden—only to be revealed by rearranging their sequence to put like with like. In the original Thomas Text the sayings occur higgledy-piggledy, to use a homely phrase. It feels as though Thomas dictated them spontaneously just as he recalled them from memory. Only occasionally does one connect with another, when the topics are similar, as though the first reminded him of the second.

So this is not an inherent feature of the teaching technique of Jesus. But their orderly sequence having now been discovered and as it is presented in this book, it is a very great benefit to us.

It is not possible to tell whether Thomas intended this second level of hiding. Probably not. In his years as a companion of Jesus he would have assimilated these Teachings, to the extent of being able to decide which sayings were to be recorded. It may well have been not important for him to marshal the sayings to emphasise the Teachings, for it would be these that he proclaimed in his missionary activity.

Thus, for one who has the urge, Jesus requires some effort to be made to discern the inner meanings of the sayings or Teachings. For some that meaning—always at a higher or deeper level—will come easily, perhaps as a kind of flash of illumination inwardly. For others the work may need profound contemplation or may extend over several years, so that it may be said that time is a major ingredient in coming to the awareness. It follows that for any person who approaches these sayings in a hurry, or with a quizzical mind, or with scepticism, or using only the intellect, the inner meanings will be blocked off, and he or she will not find what Jesus has to offer here.

The ancient Thomas Text is made available photographically in 'The Facsimile Edition of the Nag Hammâdi Codices', Brill, 1974 to 1978. With an 'Introduction' volume. Complemented by a series of volumes on each of the Codices, published up to 1989. The Thomas Text is in Codex II, folios 32 – 51; on page 4 is another photograph showing the whole ancient volume opened at folios 50 and 51. (Unfortunately, the photographs of the last page of the Thomas Text are poor.)

The complete collection of documents discovered at Nag Hammâdi are made available in 'The Nag Hammâdi Library in English' edited by J M Robinson, Brill, 1977.

The source documents and main reference books used when making this translation of the Thomas Text are noted in the Acknowledgements at the end of this book.

The Thomas People

AFTER THE CRUCIFIXION of Jesus, when his eleven main disciples had gained new Courage (Acts Ch. 2) they began to spread abroad the Teachings they had been given. They allocated amongst themselves different peoples and territories to which they would go.

This is explained in an ancient document of the Syrian Church which refers to Thomas thus:

'India, and all the countries belonging to it and round it, even to the farthest sea, received the apostles' ordination to the priesthood from Judas Thomas, who was guide and ruler in the Church which he had built there, in which he also ministered.'

This acknowledges that he initiated a great gathering or spiritual community of people that at its fullest extent stretched from Egypt (otherwise the Thomas Text would not have been at the St Palamon monastery at Chenoboskia), right across the countries now Palestine and Israel, into Syria and extending to the south of India. These were the Thomas People.

The Thomas People are to be distinguished from the Gnostics. These people who existed at much the same time and place were another community deeply interested in Jesus. Their Gnostic Gospels are markedly different from the Thomas Text and the other scriptures of the Thomas People. They too were persecuted by the early Christian Church and to some extent went underground to be kept alive in secret societies. However, as we shall see, the Thomas People were more seriously dealt with, and even today many sincere Church people are uncomfortable with parts of the Thomas Text.

First Thomas went from the fertile region watered by the river Jordan, across the deserts using the great trade routes to the next fertile region to the east, the valley of the Euphrates. He came to Edessa now called Urfa. It was then an important city which, because of its splendour and the quality of its life, was known as the Athens of the East. Here, aided especially by his own disciple Adonya or Addai, he began to gather his people, who included in due course the King Abgai.

No doubt to begin with the Teachings were communicated, as a living quality, directly from one person to another. However it must have been that while in Edessa Thomas sought out the scribe in the market place to dictate his recollected sayings of Jesus, to create the first written Thomas Text, the primary scripture of the Thomas People, for scholars generally consider it was written there.

We shall see that by 46 A.D. Thomas may have left Edessa for distant places, where it is hardly conceivable he could have dictated his Text. Therefore the Thomas Text would come from very early after the mission of Jesus, within perhaps only about a single decade.

Soon the growing community based on Edessa added another scripture, a forerunner or prototype of the Gospel of Matthew, referred to by scholars as proto-Matthew although it has also been called the Gospel of the Hebrews.* There are references to this in ancient literature, but the full text no longer exists.

In due course a hierarchy of leaders was established in order to form a structured Church. One of the scriptures important to that Syrian Church was the Diatessaron of Titian written in about 170 A.D. This was a kind of amalgam or composite of the four Gospels of the Bible, together with a fifth source probably the Thomas Text. It has been subject to frequent amendment by redactors, a particular effect being to bring it more into harmony with the canonical Gospels.

---

* It seems that Hebrews contained much that is in our Matthew's Gospel, while omitting some (for it was about 90% the length), contained text that was removed from our Matthew, and had passages similar or identical to those in the Thomas Text.

THE THOMAS PEOPLE

Titian's Diatessaron became the primary gospel used in the Syrian Church, and a major basis of the doctrines and teaching of that Church. Especially in the earlier versions of the Diatessaron a special use of the Biblical Greek word sōzō and its derivatives has been noted. Instead of this being 'to save', 'salvation' and 'the saviour', Syrian words meaning 'to live', 'life' and 'the life giver' are used; so Jesus is spoken of as the Life Giver, meaning in the here and now.

Few of the documents of that Church remain, and then usually in the form of copies from many centuries later. These have been subjected to changes by successive redactors, but it is nevertheless possible to discern a coherent and consistent teaching of that Church. These documents are known as The Acts of Thomas, the Hymn of the Pearl, and the Book of Thomas. It is considered that these were written during the period 150 to 350 A.D., and almost certainly in Syriac. The first two are now known in Syriac and Greek forms; the Book of Thomas was discovered in a Coptic version in the Nag Hammâdi Library.

The Acts of Thomas, like many other Acts of apostles or early saints, tell of the events and teachings of Thomas after he had begun his missionary activity. They tell of many episodes in the life of Thomas, incorporate concepts and even quotations from his Text, and give valuable insights into the rites of that early Church. Thus, adult baptism preceded by an anointing was the chief rite, and the eucharist took more the form of a love feast after an occasion of worship, apparently similar to that of the Sikh Church today.

In the thirteenth century the famous cathedral at Chatres in France was built to portray, by means of statues and stained glass windows, the chief events and doctrines of the Christian Church. It is a visual Teaching, for the many pilgrims visiting it who could not read. One of the windows comprises episodes that occur only in the Acts of Thomas. So not only was that known there at that date but also, and more surprisingly, reference to the Acts of Thomas was permitted by the Catholic Church.

The inspired members of that early Church initiated by Thomas later produced many texts of high mystical content. The writings of Makarios displayed the flowering of the mystical Church of Edessa. The Acts of Thomas as we now have it has interpolated into it a particularly beautiful and meaningful poem, the Hymn of the Pearl. In the book this appears at a stage in Thomas's mission when he was established in north India, at the court of King Gundaphoros.

The Hymn tells, in a form that could be chanted or even sung to music, the story of a prince living where the fertile valleys of the Euphrates and Tigris lead toward the Persian Gulf. A wonderful garment had been taken away from him, and to recover it he had to make the long journey by sea to Egypt, to search there for a pearl hidden in the Labyrinth near the pyramids, a place which mythically represented confusion and loss. Stupefied by the strange food and rigours of the search, he nearly gave up and lay down to sleep. His parents, discerning this from afar, sent to him an ambassador with a message that galvanized him to action. He found the pearl and aided by a 'female being' returned to his home—

> 'But I could not recall my splendour;
> for, it was while I was still a boy and quite young
> that I had left it behind in my father's palace.
> But suddenly when I saw my garment reflected
>   as in a mirror,
> I perceived it was my whole Self as well,
> and through it I recognized and saw myself.
> For, though we derived from one and the same
> we were partially divided;
> and then again we were One, with a single form.'

So here is a particularly vivid and beautiful presentation of the key proclamation, given in many great spiritual teachings of the world, that a person, filled with the urge to find Truth, may start by searching outside, turning this way and that, but in the end recognizes that it not only lies within but has always lain within, previously unseen.

Returning to Thomas himself, the Acts of Thomas clearly speak of Jesus surviving his crucifixion, being helped in his recovery by the Essenes of Quamran—the figures in white of John 20:12—who were skilled in medicine. This links up with twentieth century investigations showing Jesus going to Kashmir to continue his Ministry.* One of the first episodes concerning Thomas was that Jesus put him in the charge of a sea captain for a voyage to north India. It is known that at 46 A.D. King Gundaphoros ruled in the Indus valley, and Thomas became attached to his court as architect and carpenter to build a palace for the king. Thomas continued to spread the Teaching he had been given, and there are references to occasions when Jesus met up with him there.

A very strong tradition, still strongly held today, in the south of India is that Thomas came there in 52 A.D. At that time trade winds had been recently discovered which expedited voyages between the Euphrates valley and the Malabar Coast of southwest India, now Kerala. He landed at the city of Cochin, where there had been for more than a century a Jewish community who built the largest and oldest synagogue still existing. Over several years he set up churches in seven towns that can still be identified and located. Later he travelled over the mountains to the southeast of India, where he continued to widen his community of the Thomas People. He was ultimately martyred at Madras, where great gatherings are still held each year to honour him.

---

* See for example 'Jesus Lived in India', Holger Kersten (Element Books, 1986). Kersten travelled extensively in Kashmir, finding many references to teachings similar to those of Jesus, by one there named Issa. He even shows a tomb where the body of Jesus was finally laid to rest, guarded still by generations of a family.

Also 'A Search for the Historical Jesus', Fida Hassnain (Gateway Books, 1994). Professor Hassnain is Director of Museums and Antiquities for Kashmir, and extensively reviews ancient documents in that country about Jesus. Here Jesus is named Yazu Asaph. He quotes extensively yet tantalizingly from 'The Crucifixion by an Eye-Witness' (Indo-American Book Co, Chicago, 1907). He even found and quotes the recipe for the healing balm put on Jesus' wounds after his crucifixion. Very many other relevant books are referenced. He several times laments that in recent years worthy Churchmen have removed ancient documents, differing from the Church's doctrines, from his country.

Thomas's work there led to the establishment of the Orthodox Church of Thomas. This is to be distinguished from the Catholic and Protestant Churches in Kerala, all of much more recent date. That Thomas Church in the early centuries allied itself with the Syrian Church. After some time it became weak and its message diffused. However today it is vigorous, with a large number of members and many churches and shrines all in good condition.

During the great struggles for power and influence between the early Christian Churches, which came to a climax during the fourth and fifth centuries, the Syrian Church and its derivatives passed into the background as far as the Churches of the west and the Russias were concerned. And the primitive Church that was the bearer of an independent tradition to that Syrian Church (however much it may have been modified subsequently) was extinguished. That extinction was so ruthless, so thorough, that only faint traces of it remain, needing all the resources of the latest scholarship to reveal. But the Thomas Text, dug up from the sand, shines like a beacon to confirm the basic Teachings on which it was built.

Thus it may truly be said that the sayings of Jesus recorded in the Thomas Text, when their inner meanings were known, had the power to gather a great spiritual people.

G Quispel, 'Gnostic Studies', especially vol. II, 1975, Instambul.
W H C Frend, 'The Rise of Christianity', 1975, London.
A Roberts and J Darlington, 'The Ante-Nicene Fathers', vol. VIII, Edinburgh, 1968. The quotation at the start of this chapter comes from this.
M R James, 'The Apocryphal New Testament', 1953, Oxford. The quotation from the Song of the Pearl is from his translation.
E Hennecke, 'New Testament Apocrypha', tr. R McL Wilson, 1963, London.
Bentley Layton, 'The Gnostic Scriptures', 1987, London.
A F J Klijn, 'The Acts of Thomas', 1962, Leiden.
J Rendel Harris, 'The Diatessaron of Titian', 1890, London.
A Vööbus, 'Early Versions of the New Testament,' 1954, Stockholm.
C V Cheriyan, 'A History of Christianity in Kerala', 1973, Kottayam, India.
A S Atiya, 'A History of Eastern Christianity', 1968, London.

Literary Features

ALTHOUGH JESUS has important things to say about femininity, in the Thomas Text where both men and women are referred to he uses the masculine form of words. This convention, which may well have been more prevalent in his time and place than now, is reflected both in the Coptic original and this English translation.

A further convention adopted here is to use an initial capital letter on words that have a marked spiritual significance. On coming across one of these it may be of value to reflect that there is more-than-usual meaning.

Throughout this translation, 'shall' is used not only as the future tense, but also with its legitimate coloration of promise or assurance. This derives from its early English usage of being a command. Thus whenever this word is found due weight should be given to it so the reader may feel a sense of authority, certainty and conviction.

Jesus uses a number of concepts that are unfamiliar to us in our normal western culture. It is largely because he is dealing with spiritual Truth at a high level. It may be quite difficult to grasp these, but it behoves us to make the effort to do so in order that we may gain access to what he has to offer. One of the purposes of what is written in this present book is to help the awareness of these concepts.

For some of these concepts, and for certain other instances, no word in the English language exists. Therefore here foreign words are employed. Some of these are taken from the Greek or Coptic originals, although spelled with our familiar letters, while occasionally a word from a different spiritual tradition has been employed. It is found to be very much better to use these foreign words, and gradually come to understand their meanings, rather than use English renderings that can only be inadequate or misleading.

One of the distinctive features of the Thomas Text is that it uses words very precisely. That is to say, each and every word carries exactly its own meaning, there is no fuzziness or ambiguity. This is only to be expected from the words of a Master. In carrying through the translation into English great care has been taken to respect and reflect this feature.

On the other hand, there are numerous occasions when Jesus has used synonyms, usually in each case with a slightly different nuance or associated meaning involved. The most striking of these is when he is referring to the most fundamental feature of this Teaching—the nature of Spiritual Truth. In the Thomas Text he also uses for this the All, One, Unity, the Kingdom, Life, the Living, the Father, Kingdom of the Father, the Father and the Mother, Light, the Pure Spirit, Kingdom of the heavens.

Part of this precise use of words, combined with many instances of synonyms, derives from the fact that Jesus was sometimes speaking to Jewish people and at other times to the Hellenist people who comprised nine out of ten of the population of his time and place. These people used a form of the Greek language (called koine) less sophisticated than that used in the city states of Greece, lived in a society and environment largely influenced by Greek practices, were familiar with Greek concepts and ways of thinking and, in particular, knew the meaning of distinctive Greek words. We must assume that Jesus had the ability to be bilingual in his mother-tongue Aramaic and also in koine Greek. It is apparent that Jesus adapted his speech, and especially the use of important or key-words, to suit his listeners on each occasion.

During the centuries when the Thomas Text was generally available amongst the Thomas People, its probable use was to be referred to or quoted from by persons who had already grasped its inner meanings when instructing those others seeking to

LITERARY FEATURES

learn Jesus' Teachings. This practice of aspirants sitting at the feet of a Master was current in other groups at that time and is still followed amongst Hassidic Jews, Sufi Moslems and most spiritual communities of the East. This has the benefit—it might be said the vital quality—that spiritual Truth is communicated as a living quantity.

The individual sayings, taken a few at a time, and expanded upon by a Master would be an ideal medium for conveying Jesus' Teachings.

Because it has been found that a hand-written form conveys the meanings of the sayings and the Teachings more readily, the Thomas Text is here presented in fine calligraphy. Likewise, benefit will result from copying out in longhand those sayings that particularly appeal.

In the presentation here each saying is given as a series of phrases. These simulate the cadences and structure of spoken words, especially that of the original Semitic thought and speech. They can suggest the rhythm and emphasis, making use of the punctuation that has been added. It will be found beneficial to read these phrases aloud, giving a natural emphasis, and allowing plenty of time for the meaning of the words to be absorbed. The phrases follow closely the cadences of the original Coptic, and may have been a component in their use amongst the Thomas People. Furthermore, it is easy to visualize these cadences having been of value in memorizing these sayings; at a time when ordinary people could not read, this would have been the main form in which they were used by individuals.

Within the original Thomas Text as a whole, except for the initial three sayings which form a kind of summary, there is no discernable pattern to the sequence or order of the sayings. However, a feature of this presentation is to rearrange them, so as to form groups of like-with-like meanings, to reveal specific Teachings by Jesus. This virtually adds a new dimension and makes the whole far more valuable to us. It is emphasised that the hand-written pages that follow give the entire Thomas Text.

Nothing is added, nothing omitted, none of the sayings are altered. All that is done is to rearrange the sequence of the sayings in order to reveal their full significance.

Each group on a distinctive Teaching is followed, only where it seems they might be helpful, by Notes; in some cases these are expanded to become essays of spiritual import. These, set in ordinary type, are provided to help the reader find the inner meanings of the sayings and the significance of the Teachings. They provide clues, sign-posts pointing to the right direction, and guide-lines to check that a useful path is being taken. They do not attempt to give or explain the inner meanings of the sayings, for that would negate the method used by Jesus that the recipient of his sayings must do work to find the inner meanings—always at a higher or deeper level than can be set down in mere words.

For those who might have an interest in re-establishing the sequence of the sayings as they appear in the original Thomas Text, an index is provided on page 150 to simplify such reconstruction.*

---

* Alternatively, an attractive presentation of the Gospel of Thomas in its original sequence, is given in a limited hand made and hand bound edition by The Millrind Press, ISBN 1-902194-02-0. From John Kay, 22 Hall Road, Fordham, Colchester CO6 3NQ

Relationship with the Bible

A QUESTION THAT perhaps readily arises is: What is the relationship between the Thomas Text and the gospels of the Bible? It turns out that to answer that it is useful to use two of the Teachings in the Thomas Text itself.

It will be shown later that the first of these Teachings—and in fact the initial one in this present book—is the importance of discrimination in spiritual matters. That is to say, to develop the art or skill of being able to distinguish between one topic and another when they have something in common. To a large extent it involves clear thinking.

When applied to the question at the head of this chapter the discrimination means to distinguish between the narrative accounts and the records of the words of Jesus. The Thomas Text is practically devoid of narrative or descriptive passages; those that do occur, and they are very brief, merely serve to set the scene for some of the recorded sayings.

The gospels of the Bible, on the other hand, can be read to give a very substantial picture of the actions of Jesus, of situations in which he was involved, and of the reactions of people to his presence.

A second Teaching in the Thomas Text can then be applied. It will also be shown later that Jesus considered it important that he should be seen properly. In other words, that his spiritual qualities should be recognized, for which we have a third or inner spiritual eye. We all have this capability, even if all too often it may lie blinkered. Therefore when reading the narrative passages in the gospels of the Bible, the clue is to seek answers to the question: From the reactions of the people around Jesus in each episode or situation, what was it they saw with their inner eye?

RELATIONSHIP WITH THE BIBLE

A fair amount of work is needed when using the Bible in this way, and it may be found beneficial to study also the writings of enlightened commentators.*

If we now return to that initial question, the sayings in the Thomas Text may be compared with sayings of Jesus in the Bible. This is a topic of much interest to Bible scholars, and whole books have been written on the subject.

Out of the 114 sayings in the Thomas Text about sixty two of them bear some relation to those in the Bible in one way or another—some in whole or part, some closely similar and others relying on only few words in common. What is much more valuable, of course, is the remaining fifty two sayings that are entirely different from those in the Bible.

When those sayings that are related are considered as a whole, three conclusions become apparent. First, it is clear that sayings in the Thomas Text were not copied into the Bible; nor the other way around. With a little practice is becomes quite easy to detect when one text has been copied from another; not only do the subjects agree but also the actual words and their arrangement fit together. This does not happen here. Therefore it is clear that the Thomas Text and the Bible are independent. It is well known that when the gospels of the Bible were being written, there were sources, either documents or things remembered, that were available; in fact Luke specifically tells us so in Luke 1:1 – 4. When there is some relation between sayings in the Thomas Text and those in the Bible these must have come from such alternative sources.

The second conclusion relates to the sayings of Jesus generally being in the nature of parables, or at least using symbolic imagery or language—which has the power to reach to a higher level within the recipient. In the Thomas Text these inner meanings are usually not easy to discern from our ordinary standpoint, and in some instances require a real effort. The gospels of the Bible, on the other hand, were written for and

---

* For example, the books by Maurice Nicol 'The New Man' and 'The Mark' have been found very helpful.

within a growing Church that attached great importance to being catholic, in the sense of being for everyone. Therefore many instances may be noted where words have been changed to make the sayings easier to grasp. This, however, has had the effect of weakening the impact of the sayings as they occur in the Thomas Text, of blunting their cutting edge.

The third conclusion that can be noted when comparing related sayings in the Thomas Text and in the Bible is that there are some instances where substantial additions have been made, which appear to have the purpose of supporting doctrines that were being developed in the early Christian Church. This may be well illustrated by the parable of the Fisherman, an example which is often taken by scholars when making these comparisons. Here it is in the Thomas Text:

*The Man is like a wise fisherman
who cast his net into the sea;
he drew it up from the sea full of small fish.
Amongst them, he found a single large and good fish.
That wise fisherman, he cast all the small fish
        down to the bottom of the sea,
he chose the large fish without difficulty.
He who has ears to hear let him hear!*

It will be shown later that in this parable there are two inner meanings of spiritual significance. In the first, it is a wise fisherman, and he chooses the large fish without difficulty. This relates to the Teaching of Jesus—shared with many other spiritual teachers—that it is necessary to develop discrimination, the ability to discern the distinctions between what is helpful and important, and what is not. Secondly, he chooses the one large fish. This is a pointer to a teaching about the One and Oneness, which uses a Greek concept related to spiritual Truth.

When this parable appears in the Gospel of Matthew (13:47 – 50) it reads:

Again, the kingdom of heaven is like a net which was thrown into the sea and gathered fish of every kind; when it was full, men drew it ashore and sat down and sorted the good into vessels but threw away the bad. So it will be at the close of the ages. The angels will come out and separate the evil from the righteous, and throw them into the furnace of fire; there men will weep and gnash their teeth.

Note that this is no longer related to a wise fisherman, but the centre of attention has been transferred to a net. There is no emphasis on a discerning choice but instead only a common-sense process of selection of good and bad groups. So both the spiritual teachings have disappeared. Further, there follows a substantial addendum which is all related to doctrines being evolved in the early Church about the end of the world, dividing the wicked and the just, and the torments of hell fire—all totally alien to the Teachings in the Thomas Text.

It is not intended in this book to embark on a detailed review of the various examples of related sayings in the Thomas Text and the Bible. Instead, the table on the two following pages provides the references to all the examples—established by eminent Bible scholars—to aid the reader make such comparisons for himself. In the right-hand column a system of star gradings has been added to identify those examples considered of greater or lesser significance.

When one embarks on making such comparisons one may well have the experience that this is a progressively less satisfying undertaking. It may be found to have the strange feature that the further one goes the less clear are any conclusions to be drawn. In actual fact, what is happening is that the evidence for the independence of the Thomas Text is being marshalled. Therefore, in particular, one may come to the feeling that all the effort is not contributing to a greater appreciation of the spiritual values inherent in the sayings in the Thomas Text.

The passage from Matthew is quoted from the Revised Standard Version of the New Testament.

RELATIONSHIP WITH THE BIBLE

Cross-references to equivalent passages in books of the New Testament

Logion	Mark	Matthew	Luke	John	Other	Significance
3.7			17:21			★★★
4.3–5		11:25–26	10:21			★
.7–8	10:31	19:30	13:30			★
5.3–4	4:22		8:17			★★
		10:26	12:2			★★
8		13:47–50				★★★★
	particularly the absence of the addendum used by Matthew					
9	4:1–9	13:1–9	8:4–8			
	4:13–20	13:18–23	8:11–15			★★★
10			12:49–50			★
13.4–5	8:27–30	16:13–20	9:18–21			★★★★
.23–26		19:40				★
14.8–13	6:10–11	10:11–14	10:5–11			★
.13–16	7:15	15:11				★
16		10:34–36	12:51–53			★★
17		13:14–17	10:23–24		1 Cor 2:9	★
18	9:1	16:28	9:27			★
20	4:30–32	13:31–32	13:18–19			★★
21.2–4		11:16–17	7:31–32			★
.13–20		24:43–44	12:39–40			★★
22.1–4	10:13–15	19:13–14	18:15–17			★
	10:15	18:3				
.13	10:6–9	19:4–6				★★★
24.6–9		6:22–23	11:34–36	12:36		★★★
25	12:28–34	22:34–40	10:25–28			★
26		7:3–5	6:41–42			★
31	6:4–5	13:57–58	4:24			★
32.2–5		5:14				★
.3–4		7:24–27	6:47–49			★
33.1–4		10:27	12:3			★
.5–6		5:15–16	11:33			
		4:21	8:16			★★
34		15:14	6:39			★★★
35	3:27	12:29				★★
38			17:22			★
39.2–6		23:13	11:52–54			★★
.7–8		10:16	10:3			★
41		13:12	19:26			
		25:29				
		4:25	8:18			★
44	3:28–30	12:31–32	12:10			★★
45.2–4		7:16–20	6:43–45			★
.5–11		12:33–37				★★

Logion	Mark	Matthew	Luke	John	Other	Significance
46	11:11	7:28–30				★★
47.1–8		6:24	16:13			★★★
.9–19	2:21–22	9:16–17	5:36–39			★★★
		addition at Luke 5:39 inverts the meaning				
48.2–3		18:19				★★★
.4–5		17:20	(17:6)			
	11:22–23	21:21				
53					Rom 2:25,29	★
54		5:3	6:20			★★
55		10:37–38	14:26–27			★★
	8:34–35	16:24–25	9:23–24			
57		13:24–30				★★
		13:36–43				
58		5:10				★★
		10:39	17:35	12:25		
	8:35–37	16:25–26	9:24–25			
61.2–3		24:40–41	17:34–35			★
62.4–6		6:3–4				★
63			12:16–21			★★
64		22:1–10	14:15–24			★★
65	12:1–9	21:33–41	20:9–16			★★
66	12:10–11	21:42–43	20:17–18			★
68		5:11	6:22			★★★
69.6–7		5:6	6:21			★
72			12:13–15			★
73		9:37–38	10:2			★
76.2–7		13:45–46				★★
.8–12		6:19–21	12:33–34			
78		11:7–10	7:24–27			★★
79.1–6			11:27–28			★
.7–9			23:29			
86		8:19–20	9:57–58			★★★
89		23:25	11:37–40			★
90		11:28–30				★
91		16:1–3				★
93		7:6				★
96		13:33	13:20–21			★
99	3:31–35	12:46–50	8:19–20			★
100	12:13–17	22:15–22	20:20–26			★★★
104	2:18–20	9:14–15	5:33–35			★★
107		18:12–14	15:8–10			★
108.2–4			6:53 but may be out of context			★
109		13:44				★★★
113			17:20–21			★★
114		19:12 this may not be a valid equivalent				★★★

ΠΕΥΑΓΓΕΛΙΟΝ ΠΚΑΤΑΘѠΜΑC

The Good News Brought by Thomas

The title at the top is a facsimile of an exclamation at the end of the ancient book, the Thomas Text. It may have been added by the original translator, for the two letters Π are Coptic (the first meaning 'the' and the second a grammatical construction) but the rest is Greek. ΕΥΑΓΓΕΛΙΟΝ from which we get evangelist is a double-word meaning good news. ΚΑΤΑ means brought by, and we render the letter Θ by Th.

In those days news was not so much valued for its newness, but by its information-content. It was always memorized and carried by a human being, and when he delivered it he was available for a dialogue to help explain the background, its meaning and its significance. Even when a Shakespearian player exclaims "Ho, a messenger cometh" we do not expect to see a slip of paper pushed under the door!

So ΑΓΓΕΛΙΟΝ ΚΑΤΑ means information that is being brought by someone who knows its significance and can help us to understand it. Thus it is our task to bring that message alive, so it directly reaches our inner awareness.

The Summary

₁ These are the hidden logia
₂ which the living Jesus spoke
₃ and Didymos Judas Thomas wrote.

1

₁ And he said:
₂ He who finds the inner meaning of these logia
₃ will find life independent of death.

2

Jesus said:
₁ Let him who seeks not cease from seeking
₂ until he finds;
₃ and when he finds,
₄ he will be turned around,
₅ and when he is turned around
₆ he will marvel
₇ and he shall reign over the All.

3

1. *Jesus said:*
2. *If those who guide your Being say to you:*
3. *"Behold the Kingdom is in the heaven,"*
4. *then the birds of the sky will precede you;*
5. *if they say to you: "It is in the sea,"*
6. *then the fish will precede you.*
7. *But the Kingdom is in your centre*
8. *and is about you.*
9. *When you Know your Selves*
10. *then you will be Known,*
11. *and you will be aware that you are*
12. *the sons of the Living Father.*
13. *But if you do not Know yourselves*
14. *then you are in poverty,*
15. *and you are the poverty.*

It is a characteristic of oriental books that the author thinks out a summary of what he has to say, and presents it at the start. The example we are all most familiar with is the Prelude, unsurpassed in all literature, to the Gospel of John—"In the Beginning was the Word . . ."

In this respect the Thomas Text is oriental. However, western readers are accustomed to the Greek structure of a text, which starts from small beginnings and finally builds up to the conclusion of what the author has to say.

So in this present book the summary, on the previous two pages, will be repeated at the end, when the reader will be ready to discern its inner meanings and its significance. Nevertheless, there is much—perhaps of more immediate interest—in these opening pages.

Saying number 0, they have been numbered by modern scholars for convenience, must be by the person who dictated the text or by an editor. Its claim that the ensuing sayings are by Jesus is not in itself conclusive. In those days it was common practice to attribute any writings to some distinguished person, and after all every open-minded person can find words and even ideas put into the mouth of Jesus in the gospels of the Bible. However, it may well be found that the sayings in the Thomas Text have a self-authenticating quality. The clue is to consider whether their high spiritual content is present in other writings of their time and place.

The natural name of Thomas was the Jewish Judas. However, as his discipleship progressed to his becoming one of the twelve apostles, he was given the names Didymos Thomas. Since both these Greek words mean twin, this must relate to some recognition, whether by Jesus or his peers, of some spiritual twin-ship to Jesus.

Saying number 1 does not claim to be by Jesus, although almost all the others do. It could well have been a comment by Thomas based on his own experience.

Saying number 2 starts us with the words of Jesus. Immediately we can see its Semitic style with short phrases, as a

THE SUMMARY

sort of hierarchy to built up intensity. Elsewhere we have an example of Jesus' teaching being expressed in the Greek idiom—his 'farewell discourses' at the Last Supper as given by John; but John was then living in the Greek-centred city of Ephesus and writing for Greeks. The contrast with the style of this Text is striking.

Saying number 3 is in three sections. In phrases 1 to 6 Jesus is light-heartedly lampooning certain false teachers. Phrases 7 to 12 lie at the heart of the Teaching in the Thomas Text; we shall have to come to that later. The remaining phrases provide a contrast to it. The point to notice here is that the key-word used is 'Kingdom'. This carried meaning for Jewish listeners to Jesus. But in this Thomas Text it is a synonym for the 'All' used in the last line of saying 2. That word had meaning for the Hellenist listeners to Jesus. Another synonym, used elsewhere, is the 'Light'. What it reveals is that Jesus used words appropriate to his listeners on each occasion.

Just the same happens at the end of saying 3. Darkness, blindness, drunkenness, impoverishment, are all synonyms in this ancient Text.

Discrimination

8
1. And he said:
2. The Man is like a wise fisherman
3. who cast his net into the sea;
4. he drew it up from the sea full of small fish.
5. Amongst them,
6. he found a single large and good fish.
7. That wise fisherman, he cast all the small fish down to the bottom of the sea,
8. he chose the large fish without trouble.
9. He who has ears to hear let him hear!

107
1. Jesus said:
2. The Kingdom is like a shepherd
3. who owned a hundred sheep.
4. One among them, which was the largest, went astray;

DISCRIMINATION

(107)
5 he left the ninety-nine,
6 he sought after the one
7 until he found it.
8 When he had toiled,
9 he said to that sheep:
10 I desire you more than the ninety-nine!

76
1 Jesus said:
2 The Kingdom of the Father is like a man, a merchant,
3 who owned merchandise,
4 and found a pearl.
5 That merchant was wise:
6 he sold the merchandise,
7 he bought this one single pearl for himself.
8 You also, seek after the treasure
9 which does not perish,
10 which remains in the place
11 where no moth comes near to devour,
12 and no worm destroys.

36

1 Jesus said:
2 Have no care, from morning until evening
3 and from evening until morning,
4 for what you will put on.

14

1 Jesus said to them:
2 If you fast you will do
3 something prejudicial to yourselves,
4 and if you pray
5 you will be condemned,
6 and if you give alms
7 you will do harm to your spirits.
8 And as you go into every land
9 and wander in the countryside,
10 if they receive you,
11 eat what they set before you,
12 heal the sick amongst them.
13 For what goes into your mouth
14 will not defile you,
15 but what comes out of your mouth,
16 that is what will defile you.

DISCRIMINATION

89
1 *Jesus said:*
2 *Why do you wash the outside of the cup?*
3 *Do you not understand*
4 *that He who made the inside*
5 *is also He who made the outside.*

It is an element of several spiritual teachings to emphasize the need for discrimination—to attain the capability to discern the important from the unimportant, the valuable from the worthless, the good from the poor. It will be shown that many of Jesus' ideas were new, and even now are different from the doctrines of the Church. He is here urging us to approach them with discernment.

Discrimination has three components: when two things or situations appear the same but are really different, to be able to see the difference; to be able to discern the reason that they are different; and where one is more beneficial, to be able to choose it.

In some teachings discrimination is the first thing to be taught, as all else depends on it. Jesus gave several sayings to emphasise its importance. Some present simple practical episodes, behind which we are shown the working of the spiritual quality of discrimination.

In developing this faculty it is of great value to be able to turn, for guidance, to one who can serve in any particular situation as a touchstone, as a guiding star. For this it may be best to learn to see the Master.

Seeing the Master

5
1. Jesus said:
2. Know Him who is before your face,
3. and what is hidden from you shall be revealed
to you:
4. for there is nothing hidden that shall not be
manifest.

17
1. Jesus said:
2. I will give you what no eye has seen,
3. and what no ear has heard,
4. and what no hand has touched,
5. and what has not arisen in the heart of man.

15

1. Jesus said:
2. When you behold
3. Him who was not begotten of woman,
4. prostrate yourselves upon your face
5. and worship him;
6. that one is your Father.

59

1. Jesus said:
2. Look upon Him who is living
3. as long as you live,
4. lest you should die
5. and you should seek to see Him;
6. and you would not be able to see.

79
A woman from the multitude said to him:
Fortunate is the womb that bore you
and the breasts that nourished you.
He said to her:
Fortunate are they who have heard the Logos
of the Father,
and have kept it in truth.
For there will be days when you will say:
Fortunate is the womb that did not conceive
and the breasts that did not suckle.

82
Jesus said:
He who is near to me is near to the fire,
and he who is far from me is far from the
Kingdom.

77

1. *Jesus said:*
2. *I am the light that is above them all.*
3. *I am the All.*
4. *The All comes forth from me,*
5. *and the All reaches towards me.*
6. *Cleave the wood, I am there;*
7. *lift up the stone,*
8. *and you shall find me there.*

108

1. *Jesus said:*
2. *He who drinks from my mouth*
3. *shall become as me;*
4. *and I myself will become him,*
5. *and the hidden things shall be manifested.*

13

1. Jesus said to his disciples:
2. Make a comparison to me
3. and tell me whom I resemble.
4. Simon Peter said to him:
5. You resemble a righteous angel.
6. Matthew said to him:
7. You resemble a wise man, a philosopher.
8. Thomas said to him:
9. Master, my mouth will absolutely not permit
10. me to say you resemble anyone.
11. Jesus said:
12. I am not your Master;
13. because you have drunk,
14. you have become enlivened from the bubbling spring
15. which I have made to gush out.
16. He took him aside,
17. and spoke three logia to him.
18. Now, when Thomas had returned to his companions,
19. they questioned him:
20. What did Jesus say to you?
21. Thomas said to them:

(13)

²² If I tell you one of the logia that he said to me,
²³ you will take up stones
²⁴ and throw them against me;
²⁵ and fire will come forth from the stones
²⁶ and burn you up.

The disciples and others around him could see Jesus with their outer eyes. But in various ways he exhorted them to see him also with their inner eye. It is with our inner eye that we may come to see his reality, and thus be awakened to respond to him.

Going beyond the great affirmation of:

I am the light that is above them all (logion 77)

the promise may be reached of:

He who drinks from my mouth (logion 108).

This gives the ultimate mystical experience. Perhaps it may only be found during profound contemplation; the clue is to recognize that the feeling of his majesty and our minuscule being is a mere superimposition.

The saying that starts:

Make a comparison to me (logion 13)

is the only autobiographical one in the Thomas Text. As a true disciple Thomas would know he must record faithfully, and must not intrude elsewhere. Thomas tells of an episode that, when combined with related passages from the gospels in the Bible (Matthew 16:13, Mark 8:27, Luke 9:18), other old documents, and what can be seen today, can be very easily visualized.

After his initial ministry around the Lake of Galilee and having gathered some disciples, Jesus might have suggested a visit up the River Jordan, 70 kilometres or so through mountainous country, to its source. At that time, as now, merit attached to a journey to the source of a holy river. To accommodate the many pilgrims, Proconsul Hadrian had enhanced a village nearby, in the country of the Phillipians, but by naming it after the Roman Caesar he angered the Jews.

Around the source there have been through the ages small shrines or monuments to sacred figures, philosophers and wise men. At this stage the stature of Jesus had not yet been recognized, even by all the disciples. But looking round him he might well have asked whom he resembled. The replies of Peter and Matthew might have been prompted by the small shrines on either hand. However, Thomas had beheld him, with awe and wonder—incomparable. Immediately Jesus implied that in a certain sense the experience of Oneness made something common to both the disciple and to the Source.

The source itself of the Jordan is a powerful spring that gushes, bubbling, out of the clefts in the rock at this place. The significance of the dialogue with Thomas that follows is heightened by the newness of the water of the spring, that this spring and the Jordan is the only river in Palestine that flows continuously through the year, and by the immense historical and spiritual importance of the Jordan to anyone born a Jew.

There then develops a situation of a type that is well authenticated in other situations: Jesus could discern the spiritual capability of a follower, and, taking him aside, gave a facet of Truth that others were not yet ready to grasp. We cannot tell what Jesus said. But it is very clear that Jesus taught his chosen disciple something that he and his colleagues considered to be blasphemous and punishable by ritual stoning, and had the power to set the world on fire. There is not much likelihood that the others would wish to record this. How could anyone other than he who had this daunting experience recount it, or feel it important to record it? It can only be the way Thomas put his 'signature' to his Text—for those with eyes to see it.

Perhaps today, for anyone brought up in the Jewish or Christian Churches, Jesus might still be speaking what appears to be a blasphemy.

In seeking to see Jesus it is of inestimable value—in fact it may be said to be essential—also to consider the incidents and episodes concerning Jesus narrated in the gospels of the Bible. Perhaps because these are less direct or specific than the sayings attributed to him, it does seem that they may have been less influenced by the doctrines of the emerging Christian Church. When working on the meaning, import or significance of these narrated episodes, the clue is to seek an answer to the question: from the reaction of the disciples or other persons what quality in Jesus did they see?

Turning to the Master

101
1. He who does not turn away from his father and his mother
2. in my way
3. will not be able to become my disciple;
4. and he who does not love his Father and his Mother
5. in my way
6. will not be able to become my disciple;
7. for my mother has begotten me
8. but my true Mother gave me _Life_.

104
1. They said to him:
2. Come and let us pray today and let us fast!
3. Jesus said:
4. What therefore is the sin that I have committed
5. or in what have I been overcome?
6. But when the bridegroom comes forth from the bridal chamber
7. then let them fast and let them pray.

100

1. They showed Jesus a gold coin
2. and said to him:
3. Caesar's agents demand taxes from us.
4. He said to them:
5. Give the things of Caesar to Caesar,
6. give the things of God to God,
7. and that which is mine, give to me.

They showed Jesus a gold coin (logion 100) is the only reference in this Teaching to God as the word is used in the Jewish and New Testament scriptures.

Here in phrases 5 to 7 is another hierarchical sequence of phrases, of increasing significance. The conclusion to be drawn is startling.

To Know and Metanoïa

3
1. Jesus said:
2. If those who guide your Being say to you:
3. "Behold the Kingdom is in the heaven,"
4. then the birds of the sky will precede you;
5. if they say to you: "It is in the sea,"
6. then the fish will precede you.
7. But the Kingdom is in your centre
8. and is about you.
9. When you Know your Selves
10. then you will be Known,
11. and you will be aware that you are
12. the sons of the Living Father.
13. But if you do not Know yourselves
14. then you are in poverty,
15. and you are the poverty.

5

1. Jesus said:
2. Know Him who is before your face,
3. and what is hidden from you shall be revealed to you:
4. for there is nothing hidden that shall not be manifest.

46

1. Jesus said:
2. From Adam until John the Baptist,
3. among the children begotten of women
4. there is none higher than John the Baptist,
5. such that his vision will be able to see Truth.
6. But I have said:
7. He who amongst you becomes as a child
8. shall Know the Kingdom,
9. and he shall be higher than John.

69

1 Jesus said:
2 Happy are they
3 who have been pursued in their heart.
4 It is they
5 who have Known the Father in Truth.
6 Happy are they who are hungry,
7 so that the belly of those who desire
        to see Truth shall be satisfied.

78

1 Jesus said:
2 Why did you come forth to the country?
3 To see a reed shaken by the wind
4/5 and to see a man clothed in soft garments?
6 See, your kings and your nobles;
7 these are clothed in soft garments,
8 and they will not be able to Know the Truth.

105

1. Jesus said:
2. He who knows the Father and the Mother,
3. will be beyond all worldly parentage.

91

1. They said to him:
2. Tell us who you are
3. so that we may believe in you.
4. He said to them:
5. You scrutinize the face of heaven and earth
6. and him who is before you
7. you have not known,
8. and you know not how to probe this revelation.

28

1. Jesus said:
2. I stood boldly in the midst of the world
3. and I manifested to them in the flesh.
4. I found them all drunk;
5. I found none among them athirst,
6. and my soul was afflicted for the sons of men
7. because they are blind in their heart
8. and they do not see
9. that empty they came into the world
10. and that empty they seek to go out of the world again,
11. except that now they are drunk.
12. When they shake off their wine,
13. then they will transform their Knowing.

The verb 'to know' is the key word of this Teaching. It appears in three forms in the Coptic. Sowōn is used consistently in the Thomas Text with the meaning of a profound certainty known at the depth of one's being. It is as when we say "I know that I am myself and no-one else". It is rendered here with an initial capital letter.

When spelt soown it is used consistently in the Coptic with lesser significance. It is here rendered variously, as 'to realize', 'to recognize', 'to understand', or 'to know' as when we say "I know it is raining".

The third form eime is lighter still, and is rendered as 'to be aware', as when we say "I am aware that there are many religions in the world".

TO KNOW AND METANOÏA

In *Tell us who you are* (logion 91) there is, in phrase 3, the only occurrence of the word 'believe', and it is used by disciples from the Hebrew background. In this Teaching, Jesus never uses nor refers to the concept of belief, or of believing, or of believers.

Likewise, nowhere in this Teaching is there reference to faith, to having faith, to being one of the faithful.

Instead, the key concept of the Teaching is to know—spiritual Truth being something that is found and known.

Metanoïa used in the heading to this chapter is a double Greek word. The meta- part means to transform, as in our metamorphosis when a chrysalis transforms into a butterfly. However the second part is much more subtle and meaningful. As Jesus uses it in the Thomas Text in the final phrase and word of:

> ... *When they shake off their wine,*
> *then they will transform their Knowing.* (logion 28)

he is using it in the sense of the Coptic sowōn, a very fundamental Knowing at the centre of one's Being. Such metanoïa will transform men from spiritual blindness and drunkenness—which gravely afflicted Jesus—into those Knowing spiritual Light and Life.

Metanoïa is obviously profoundly important, even though Jesus uses the word only once in the Thomas Text. However it can be seen that the word itself was important for Jesus, for he uses it many times in the ancient Greek versions of the gospels of the Bible.

Unfortunately, it might almost be called a calamity, from the Middle Ages and still to this day metanoïa in the words of Jesus in the Bible has been mistranslated as to repent. Repenting and repentance involves a negative emotion, and looking to the past, seeing deeds or thoughts from that spiritual darkness. That is just the opposite of all that Jesus is offering in the Thomas Text, a positive way forward to the Light.

Birth and Death

18
1. The disciples said to Jesus:
2. Tell us in what way our end will be.
3. Jesus said:
4. Have you therefore discerned the beginning
5. since you seek after the end?
6. For in the Place where the beginning is,
7. there will be the end.
8. Happy is he who will stand boldly at the beginning,
9. he shall Know the end,
10. and shall find Life independent of death.

BIRTH AND DEATH

19
1 **Jesus said:**
2/3 **Happy is he who already was before he is.**
4 **If you become my disciples**
5 **and hear my logia,**
6 **even these stones will minister to you.**
7 **For you have five trees in Paradise**
8 **which are unchanged in summer or winter**
9 **and their leaves do not fall away.**
10 **He who knows them**
11 **shall find _life_ independent of death.**

Jesus answers a question about death by directing us to become aware of our beginning. This topic is put near the start of this book because it affects us all; also, the responses we are given are rather spectacularly different from much in the Bible and the doctrines of the Christian Church. However some concepts here are covered further on in this book, so it may be necessary to come back to these two sayings later.

At that stage, when one is ready, take into account that the sayings in this Teaching are a whole, at least in the mind of him who said them. So look elsewhere for the meaning of Jesus' reply.

Happy is he who already was (logion 19, page 58)
If they say to you: "Where are you from?"
(logion 50, page 61)
Happy are the monakos and the chosen
(logion 49, page 108)
The man old in days will not hesitate (logion 4, page 79) (in that order) reiterate that in our beginning we come from the Light; it is inherent within us, and by seeing it we come to the Life in the here and now that is independent of the death of the body.

Thus to know rightly the beginning and the end leads to living in the present, and concern about death does not arise.

These two sayings (logia 18 and 19) deal with the happiness of knowing that one's true identity exists throughout life. It is there at the beginning (logion 4 spoke of that) and extends to the end. However, it is more than a continuity within time; more specifically the Real Self is independent of time.

Such Life is not merely immortal, but rather is outside of the concept of time, and so is independent of death.

Phrases 2 and 3 of the second of these two sayings are a prompt to take us to an awareness of an even higher level than the previous one. Whereas that directed us to disregard the beginning and the end—a duality—this refers to finding what was and is as a Oneness. The sayings heard and known inwardly by the disciple make a happy man, to whom even stones will minister, the trees of completeness are changeless through the seasons, and he finds Life independent of death.

Light at the Centre

24

1. His disciples said:
2. Show us the Place where you are,
3. because it is necessary for us to seek after it.
4. He said to them:
5. He who has ears let him hear:
6. There is Light
7. at the centre of a man of Light,
8. and he illumines the whole world.
9. If he does not shine,
10. there is darkness.

33

1. Jesus said:
2. What you will hear in one ear
3. and in the other ear,
4. that proclaim from your housetops.
5. For no one lights a lamp
6. and puts it under a bowl,
7. nor does he put it in a hidden place,

(33)
but he sets it on the lamp stand
in order that everyone who goes in and comes out
may see its light.

50
1. Jesus said:
2. If they say to you:
3. "Where are you from?"
4. say to them:
5. "We came from the Light
6. there, where the Light was,
7. by itself.
8. It stood boldly
9. and manifested itself in their image."
10. If they say to you:
11. "Who are you?"
12/13. say: "We are his sons
14. and we are the chosen of the Living Father."
15. If they question you:
16. "What is the sign of your Father in you?"
17. say to them:
18. "It is a movement with a repose."

Finding the Light at the Centre

109
1. Jesus said:
2. The Kingdom is like a man
3. who owned in his field a hidden treasure,
4. it being unknown to him.
5. He bequeathed it to his son after he died.
6. The son not knowing of it,
7. took that field
8. and sold it.
9. And he who bought it, came.
10. While ploughing, he found the treasure;
11. he began to lend money at interest
12. to whomsoever he wished.

111

1 *Jesus said:*
2 *The heavens and the earth will roll back*
3 *before you,*
4 *and he who is living, from the Living,*
5 *shall see neither death nor fear,*
6 *because Jesus said this:*
7 *For him who finds his true Self*
8 *the world of objects is of no worth.*

10

1 *Jesus said:*
2 *I have cast fire upon the world,*
3 *and behold, I guard it*
4 *until it is ablaze.*

Quenching Ahamkāra*

58
1 *Jesus said:*
2 *Happy is the man who has toiled to lose ahamkāra,*
3 *he has found the Life.*

71
1 *Jesus said:*
2 *I will overturn this house,*
3 *and no one will be able to build it again.*

---

* Ahamkāra is the name given here to a concept that is very strange to us. The concept is considered on pages 72 onwards. It is the concept that is important, not its name which is only a convenience to refer to it. The concept is the key to unlock the meanings of this important group of sayings, and many others. Without it, these sayings remain impossibly difficult.

Ahamkāra is pronounced as four quick syllables, one with long-a as in English car, the other three short.

37

1. His disciples said:
2. On which day will you be manifest to us
3. and on which day will we behold you?
4. Jesus said:
5. When you strip yourselves of your shame,
6. and take your garments
7. and put them under your feet
8. even as little children,
9. and you trample them;
10. then shall you behold the Son
11. of Him who is living,
12. and you shall not fear.

70

1. Jesus said:
2. When you bring forth that in yourselves,
3. this which is yours will save you;
4. if you do not have that in yourselves,
5. this which is not yours in you will kill you.

97

1. Jesus said:
2. The Kingdom of the Father is like a woman
3. who was carrying a jar full of flour
4. while walking on a long road;
5. the handle of the jar broke
6. the flour streamed out behind her on the road
7. As she did not know it
8. she could not be troubled by it.
9. When she had reached her house
10. she put the jar on the ground;
11. she found it empty.

98

1. Jesus said:
2. The Kingdom of the Father is like a man
3. wishing to kill a giant.
4. He drew the sword in his house,
5. he struck it through the wall
6. in order to be assured that his hand would be confident.
7. Then he slew the giant.

35

1 Jesus said:
2 It is not possible
3 for one to enter the house of the strong man
4 and take it by force
5 unless he binds his hands;
6 then he will plunder his house.

103

1 Jesus said:
2 Happy is the man who knows
3 where and when the robbers will creep in;
4 so that he will arise
5 and gather his strength
6 and prepare for action
7 before they come.

QUENCHING AHAMKĀRA

21
1. Mary said to Jesus:
2. Whom do your disciples resemble?
3. He said:
4. They resemble small children
5. dwelling in a field
6. which is not theirs.
7. When the owners of the field come,
8. they will say
9. "Release to us our field."
10. They strip off their outward façade before them
11. to release it to them
12. and to give back their field to them.
13. For this reason I say:
14. If the owner of the house is aware
15. that the thief is coming,
16. he will stay awake before he comes
17. and will not allow the thief
18. to tunnel into his house of his Kingdom
19. to carry away his goods.
20. But you, already watch the world,
21. prepare for action with great strength
22. lest the robbers should find a way
23. to come to you;

(21)
24 because the advantage that you expect,
25 they will find.
26 Let there be in your centre
27 a man who is understanding!
28 When the produce ripened
29 he came in haste, his sickle in his hand,
30 he reaped it.
31 He who has ears to hear let him hear!

61

1. Jesus said:
2. Two will rest there on a couch:
3. one will die, the other will live.
4. Salome said:
5. Who are you, man?
6. Is it even as he from the One
7. that you reclined on my couch
8. and ate at my table?
9. Jesus said to her:
10. I am He who is,
11. from Him who is the same;
12. what belongs to my Father was given to me.
13. Salome said: I myself am your disciple.
14. Jesus said to her: Because of that I say this:
15. When he is emptied
16. he will be filled with Light;
17. but when he is divided
18. he will be filled with darkness.

28

1. Jesus said:
2. I stood boldly in the midst of the world
3. and I manifested to them in the flesh.
4. I found them all drunk;
5. I found none among them athirst,
6. and my soul was afflicted for the sons of men
7. because they are blind in their heart
8. and they do not see
9. that empty they came into the world
10. and that empty they seek to go out of the world again,
11. except that now they are drunk.
12. When they shake off their wine,
13. then they will transform their Knowing.

10

1. Jesus said:
2. I have cast fire upon the world,
3. and behold, I guard it
4. until it is ablaze.

7

1. *Jesus said:*
2. *Happy is the lion which the man will eat,*
3. *and the lion will become man;*
4. *and abominated is the man whom the lion will eat,*
5. *and the lion will become man.*

42

1. *Jesus said:*
2. *Become your Real Self, as ahamkāra passes away.*

The inner meaning of this group of sayings, which is probably the most difficult in this Teaching, can only be grasped by an awareness of a concept that is virtually absent from western thought, even though it is central to several eastern spiritual teachings. It involves a spiritual Teaching at a very high level.

No European languages have a word for the concept, so it will be best to borrow an eastern word—ahamkāra. Its meaning is the dominance of the body, of the mind and its emotions, and of the individual soul. In consequence an ordinary person mistakenly identifies the self as comprising the body, mind and spirit. This dominance veils the Real Self that lies at a higher level, even though only latent or hidden within each person. The main spiritual work is to quench ahamkāra, to quench this dominance. Then the Real Self becomes spontaneously and automatically known.

Surprisingly, however, ordinary speech touches on this, but without its significance being noted. We say "my body", "my mind and thoughts", "my feelings and emotions". These phrases come entirely naturally to us; we know them to be valid without anyone having to convince us. The point is: who is it who can say "my"? It is the hidden Real Self.

The Real Self, the true Self are synonyms. So too are Reality, Truth, the Absolute, the Ultimate; and also terms used in the Thomas Text—the All, One, Unity, the Kingdom, Life, the Living, the Father, Kingdom of the Father, the Father and the Mother, Light, the Pure Spirit, Kingdom of the heavens—all these are as facets on the jewel that is this. The jewel itself is of course beyond the capability of any word or words to describe—words make up a part of it and a part cannot describe the whole.

Ahamkāra may go under other names, especially when rendered into English. Thus in Sufi literature there is the tiny poem where, as the 'little self' it is contrasted with the Real Self:

> Awhile, as wont may be,
> self I did claim;
> true Self I did not see,
> but heard its name.
> I, being self-confined,
> Self did not merit,
> till, leaving self behind,
> did Self inherit. *

Ahamkāra derives from the mind, the emotions, the body and outward material factors. Being egoistic or selfish, self-opinionated, self-assertive or competitive, possessive, proud, changeable or vacillating, distressed or sad, despairing or

---

* Jalal al Din Rumi (1207 – 1273), one of the greatest Persian Sufi poets, quoted in 'Man's Religious Quest', Unit 21, page 71, The Open University, 1978.

fearful, placing reliance on concepts or doctrines, are all manifestations of ahamkāra. Suffering, whether of the body or in the emotions, can only belong to ahamkāra—the significance of this cannot be overemphasized.

Happiness and bliss, peace and repose and tranquillity, certainty and stability and assurance and steadiness, contentment, consideration and generosity, gratitude, love and compassion, beauty, reliance, strength and fearlessness and courage, knowledge, all belong to the realm of the Real Self.

Anything seen by the Real Self is an object. So the Real Self looks on—it may be said looks down on from a higher level—the entire material and objective world. That world is seen, the Real Self is the seer.

Each of us is born free of ahamkāra, one of the special attractions of any small child. With the passing of years ahamkāra develops its domination. It is a major part of the spiritual work to overcome this. The 'temptations in the desert' we read of in Mark 1:12,13, Matthew 4:1–11, Luke 4:1–13 must be a crude and anthropomorphic reference to the final stages of Jesus quenching ahamkāra to reach the freedom from it that made him ready to start his Ministry to mankind. One could say that ahamkāra is everything that Jesus was free from. But strangely the gospels of the Bible make no further reference to this nor propound its value for us.

Ahamkāra is far more easily seen in other people than in oneself—one of its tricks. It may be of value to learn first to discern it in others, in the events and contacts of daily life, in order to be more prepared to detect it when it manifests within.

Thomas recorded many sayings in his Text that relate to ahamkāra. They may helpfully be considered in sub-groups, as Jesus worked to convey to his hearers first one and then another aspect of this concept. Thus the first of these groups comprises:

Happy is the man who has toiled to quench ahamkāra,
(logion 58)

I will overturn this house (logion 71)
When you strip yourselves of your shame (logion 37)
When you bring forth that in yourselves (logion 70)

Here Jesus is speaking succinctly of what has been written above. (In this Teaching 'house' refers to the Being of man.)

However, the last two of those sayings are somewhat difficult, so it may be helpful to have rather liberal paraphrases, as follows:

His disciples said:
On which day will you be manifest to us
and on which day will we behold you?
The Master said:
When you strip yourselves of your pride and
ostentation,
and take your outward façades
and treat them as nought
—even as do little children—
and, furthermore, scorn and discard them;
Then shall you behold the living Master,
and you shall not fear.

And for the second:

The Master said:
When you bring forth that which is inherently within
yourselves,
this which is yours will save you;
but if you do not acknowledge that within yourselves,
the invasive ahamkāra will kill you, denying access to
Truth.

... like a woman who was carrying a jar full of flour
(logion 97)
... like a man wishing to kill a giant (logion 98)

Two simple word-pictures related to situations of his day. These must have been addressed to Jewish hearers because of the use of the Kingdom of Heaven as the state to be reached by quenching ahamkāra, whether gradually throughout life as some people achieve it or by some violent action, as occurs with others.

> *It is not possible for one to enter the house of the strong man* (logion 35)
> *... knows where and when the robbers will creep in* (logion 103)
> *Whom do your disciples resemble?* (logion 21)

Here the invasive ahamkāra is likened to the strong forces within us that, like robbers or a thief, steal away our awareness of what is truly within us. This wily ahamkāra can appear in many different forms—as a strong man, as brigands, or making us live in a field not really ours. All this needs to be watched for, and demands one's strength to guard against.

> *Salome said: Who are you, man?* (logion 61)
> *I stood boldly in the midst of the world* (logion 28)

When Jesus stayed in Salome's home she, in her wonderment, came very near the limit of what a hostess might say, bordering on the impertinent. Jesus, however, was above being offended, and responded with words of great profundity. These swept through her, and it is the contrast between the arrogance of phrase 5 and the simple humility of phrase 13 expressing her discipleship that reveals the sudden collapse of her ahamkāra. Her reward, later, was to be named Salome, 'the perfect one'. The enigmatic quality of what Jesus then said to her, speaking so he could be heard by the others, vanishes by understanding "When one is emptied of ahamkāra", with the consequence and value of being thus emptied, and thereby filled undividedly with Light.

Likewise, in logion 28, Jesus was afflicted in his soul because men, in their spiritual blindness and drunkenness, do not see that they were born without ahamkāra and later seek to rid themselves of it. By finding that emptiness it will be the means to achieve metanoïa, to transform their deepest Knowing.

In effect, Jesus is saying that only when a person empties himself or herself of ahamkāra will Spiritual Truth be known. Jesus, Thomas and great saints attained this. Thus it may be said that in one's search for illumination, reading or more so hearing the words of only such a person will be of real worth.

I have cast fire upon the world (logion 10)
Happy is the lion which the man will eat (logion 7)
One meaning, at least, of the first saying is a simple assertion that the fire brought by Jesus has the capacity to burn up ahamkāra.*

The second is one of the more difficult sayings. It is in the nature of a Zen koan, where phrase 4 being the inverse or reverse of phrase 2, our ordinary mental and logical approach would expect phrases 3 and 5 also to be reversed. But, these being identical, we are challenged to rise to a higher level. The clue lies in the awareness that the lion represents ahamkāra; the Living man has assimilated this, not been consumed by it. It may also be helpful to have a more expanded paraphrase, thus:

Happy are the primaeval forces that the enlightened man will assimilate,
and they will be integrated and purified by the man;

---

* Irina Tweedie in 'The Chasm of Fire' (Element Books, 1988) tells vividly of her experience of going through the fire as her ahamkāra was quenched by a contemporary spiritual Teacher. Three times Jesus heaped fire on Peter, Matthew 16:23, Luke 22:34, logion 114 here, yet later he 'wept bitterly' Luke 22:62 and then came through it, Luke 22:32. Paul never met Jesus in person to have his ahamkāra burnt up.

> *but abominated is the ordinary man consumed by those forces,*
> and they will constitute that man.

> *Become your Real Self, as ahamkāra passes away.*
> (logion 42)

Jesus distills and crystalizes the very heart of his Teaching in this tiny saying—its brevity precludes all dross, as pure gold from the refiner's fire.

Jesus might well have given this to his closest disciples as a mantra.

In the original it comprises only three words, which can be literally translated 'Become yourselves, passing by.' However the meaning comes through better in the calligraphic form.

The intent is to prompt us—it is in the imperative—to disregard the things of the material world or of our minds and emotions, to become unattached to them. Thus, for example, to do all the outward things of living without being a 'doer'; or when troubles beset us to let them pass by; or to allow the good and pleasing things to come to us without in any way claiming them. All such attachment, or being a doer, or claiming comes from ahamkāra. Letting the dominance of that go, each of us becomes our Real Self.

Oneness

8
1. And he said:
2. The Man is like a wise fisherman
3. who cast his net into the sea;
4. he drew it up from the sea full of small fish.
5. Amongst them,
6. he found a single large and good fish.
7. That wise fisherman, he cast all the small fish down to the bottom of the sea,
8. he chose the large fish without trouble.
9. He who has ears to hear let him hear!

4
1. Jesus said:
2. The man old in days will not hesitate
3. to ask a little child of seven days
4. about the Place of Life,
5. and he will live;
6. for many who are first shall become last
7. and they shall be a single one.

ONENESS

48

1 *Jesus said:*
2 *If two make peace with each other*
3 *in this single house,*
4 *they will say to the mountain*
5 *"Move away"*
6 *and it shall move.*

106

1 *Jesus said:*
2 *When you make the two One,*
3 *you will become Sons of man,*
4 *and if you say:*
5 *"Mountain, move away,"*
6 *it shall move.*

22

1. Jesus saw children who were being suckled.
2. He said to his disciples:
3. These children who are being suckled are like
4. those who enter the Kingdom.
5. They said to him:
6. Shall we then, being children,
7. enter the Kingdom?
8. Jesus said to them:
9. When you make the two One,
10. and you make the inner as the outer,
11. and the outer as the inner,
12. and the above as the below,
13. so that you will make the male and the female
14. into a single One,
15. in order that the male is not made male
16. nor the female made female;
17. when you make eyes in place of an eye,
18. and a hand in place of a hand,
19. and a foot in place of a foot,
20. and an image in place of an image,
21. then shall you enter the Kingdom.

ONENESS

11

1. Jesus said:
2. This heaven will pass away,
3. and that which is above it will pass away,
4. and the dead do not live,
5. and the living will not die.
6. In the days you fed on what is dead,
7. you made of that, the living.
8. When you are in the light
9. what will you do!
10. On the day you were One,
11. you created the two;
12. but then being two,
13. what will you do?

87

1. Jesus said:
2. Wretched is the body that depends on a body,
3. and wretched is the soul that depends on these two.

112

1. Jesus said:
2. Woe to the flesh that depends upon the soul!
3. Woe to the soul that depends upon the flesh!

88

1. Jesus said:
2. The angels with the prophets will come to you
3. and they will give you what is yours.
4. You also, give what is in your hands
5. to them,
6. and say to yourselves:
7. On which day will they come
8. and receive what is theirs?

ONENESS

89
1 Jesus said:
2 Why do you wash the outside of the cup?
3 Do you not understand
4 that He who made the inside
5 is also He who made the outside.

30
1 Jesus said:
2 The place where there are three gods,
3 they are gods;
4 where there are two or one,
5 I myself am with him.

23
1 Jesus said:
2 I will choose you, one out of ten thousand,
3 and two out of ten thousand,
4 and they shall stand boldly being a single One.

72

1 A man said to him:
2 Tell my brothers
3 to divide my father's possessions with me.
4 He said to him:
5 Oh man, who made me a divider?
6 He turned to his disciples,
7 he said to them:
8 Is it that I am a divider?

76

1 Jesus said:
2 The Kingdom of the Father is like a man, a merchant,
3 who owned merchandise,
4 and found a pearl.
5 That merchant was wise:
6 he sold the merchandise,
7 he bought this one single pearl for himself.
8 You also, seek after the treasure
9 which does not perish,
10 which remains in the place
11 where no moth comes near to devour,
12 and no worm destroys.

ONENESS

67

1 *Jesus said:*
2 *He who understands the All,*
3 *but lacking himself*
4 *lacks everything.*

62

1 *Jesus said:*
2 *I tell my mysteries*
3 *to those who are worthy of my mysteries.*
4 *Whatever your right hand will do,*
5 *let not your left hand be aware*
6 *of what it does.*

77

1. Jesus said:
2. I am the light that is above them all.
3. I am the All.
4. The All comes forth from me,
5. and the All reaches towards me.
6. Cleave the wood, I am there;
7. lift up the stone,
8. and you shall find me there.

ONENESS

Jesus spoke many times in various ways about the One or the All. These terms are in the Greek idiom, and must have been used when he was amongst the Hellenist people. It is not difficult to see that they refer to the same thing—more strictly they both point to the same Place; either of them has to be complete, and there can only be one completeness.

We may refer to this as Oneness and at the highest level it becomes Spiritual Truth or Ultimate Reality. These sayings direct us to recognize that whenever in the spiritual a duality, a pair, is noted, with further seeking an underlying unity or over-riding Oneness may be found. To many this truism may be first experienced when a man and woman wed, and find the Oneness of marriage.

The man old in days will not hesitate (logion 4)

Not with the mind could we accept that an old man might see the essence of Life in an infant. But by going to a deeper Place within us the wonder, still unsullied, inherent within each person may be discerned.

If two make peace with each other (logion 48)
When you make the two One, (logion 106)

The mountain in these sayings is that of distress and suffering, which can only belong to the realm of ahamkāra. The two refers to ahamkāra and the Real Self. The only way ahamkāra and the Real Self can make peace with each other within one's Being, or the two be made One, is for ahamkāra to be quenched. Then the Real Self, which may be said to reside within the body and mind but not be of either, can reign alone.

Here Jesus asserts his Teaching, perhaps of paramount consequence to each man or woman in going through life, that when emptied of ahamkāra the mountain of suffering shall—it is a promise and a command—move away. His is the same objective as Buddha's, even if he reaches it by a different way.

Jesus saw children who were being suckled (logion 22) is developed into one of the greatest sayings by Jesus about Oneness, if only because it can lead us through progressively higher levels of awareness. It is a saying worth returning to, even over a period of years.

It starts with simple questions, where Jesus was amongst Jewish people, accustomed to the Aramaic idiom, who had at least discerned the unsullied quality in each of us as children. He responds in characteristically Semitic speech, yet by phrase 9 it has become necessary to move to the Greek idiom to provide the answers. Amongst the many instances of two becoming One, Unity found from duality, that in phrase 9 refers—as so often in this Teaching—to ahamkāra and the Self within each of us.

By phrase 14 maleness and femaleness have merged, or risen to a stage for which we have the word mankind. This is amplified or confirmed in phrases 15 and 16, where both the male and the female have disappeared. Perhaps it might have been the wish of Jesus that those who cry for feminism would rise to this level.

By phrase 17 we are brought up against the equivalent of a Zen koan or 'non-statement'—typical of an oriental Teacher. Our minds, following on what has gone before, wish to make this read 'when you make an [inner] eye in place of the eyes'. However the ancient Coptic is quite clear, it will not permit this. We are being forced—or at least, for those who wish to, prompted—to go beyond the mind. As we allow ourselves to move to that higher stage, to that place of the All where there is only the Ultimate, all objects, the hand, the foot and even the image, cease to exist.

Finally Jesus shows that this traverse of high spiritual Teaching can come back to the Jewish summit.

Everything above, being of the world of objects
(logion 11)
relates to the Teaching that each man is originally a Oneness, has developed a duality—largely through the concepts and doctrines

of the mind—can come back to the Unity during his life in this world, in which there is no death, and can then purify whatever he assimilates. This can be done by answer to the question: What will you do? It is a quest by the individual.

Woe to the flesh that depends upon the soul! (logion 112)

Here the flesh and the soul are a duality; so are the soul and the flesh. Within each, the two elements are linked by the mind. To be centred in the mind is a woeful state. By putting both phrases in juxtaposition, with something like a Zen koan, Jesus seeks to raise us beyond the mind, to the Place where the Being is in Oneness.

The angels and the prophets will come to you (logion 88)

His Jewish hearers were accustomed to the angels and the prophets, and knew what they could give. However, Jesus asserts that this is also possessed by the disciples. He wishes them to become aware of it, and to ask the question that will lead to knowing that these two are One.

Why do you wash the outside of the cup? (logion 89)

To take this apparently prosaic saying as a call to maintain a life of both an inner and an outer purity is again only to see the first level of meaning. The inside and the outside represent a duality, and a key teaching throughout the Thomas Text is that whenever a duality is identified there is need to seek further for a Unity above or beyond both.

He who understands the All (logion 67)

is like another Zen koan. It tries to take the seeker beyond his logical mind, to a higher level within. It may be helpful to have a paraphrase, thus:

He who would understand the All with his mind,
but if he lacks his true Self
he will be deprived of the All.

However, note that the Knowing of the Self precedes the Knowing of the All.

I tell my mysteries (logion 62)

'Mystery' (the Greek word mysthrion) does not here mean something mysterious, but the inner meaning of a saying. Jesus reveals his mysteries and hence Teachings to those ready and willing to receive them. The first sentence alerts us to a spiritual Teaching at a high level to follow.

To make the two One is to abolish the subject-object distinction. The left hand can only know what the right hand is doing through the intermediary of the mind. By going beyond the mind (logion 22 on page 81) it is reduced to silence and is suppressed; then there is simply a pure attention, without judgement on the right hand's action. By this example, Jesus teaches us how we must receive his mysteries.

I am the light that is above them all. (logion 77)

Many people find this to be one of their favourites amongst these sayings of Jesus. In phrases 6 to 9, this is not the pantheistic doctrine that there is divinity in a piece of wood or stone, but an encouragement that the world of objects may, when rightly viewed, point us to the Ultimate.

Spiritual Life Essential

40
1. Jesus said:
2. A vine was planted without the Father
3. and being not made firm,
4. it will be pulled up by its roots
5. and perish.

41
1. Jesus said:
2. He who has in his hand,
3. to him shall be given;
4. and he who does not have,
5. even the little that he has
6. shall be taken from him.

45

1 Jesus said:
2 Grapes are not harvested from thorn trees
3 nor are figs gathered from thistles,
4 for these give no fruit.
5 A good man brings forth good from his storehouse,
6 a bad man brings forth ill
7 from his wicked storehouse
8 which is in his heart,
9 and he speaks ill:
10 for out of the abundance of the heart
11 he brings forth ill.

44

1 Jesus said:
2 He who blasphemes against the Father,
3 it shall be forgiven him,
4 and he who blasphemes against the Son,
5 it shall be forgiven him;
6 but he who blasphemes against the pure Spirit,
7 it shall not be forgiven him, neither on earth nor in heaven.

From Small Things Great Grow

9

1. Jesus said:
2. Behold, the sower went out.
3. He filled his hand and threw.
4. Some seeds indeed fell on the road;
5. the birds came and plundered them.
6. Others fell on the rock
7. and did not take root in the earth
8. nor did they send up their heads to the sky.
9. And others fell on thorn trees;
10. these choked the seeds
11. and the worms ate them.
12. Others fell on good earth,
13. which brought forth good produce to the sky;
14. it bore sixty per measure
15. even one hundred and twenty per measure.

20

1. *The disciples said to Jesus:*
2. *Tell us, what is the Kingdom of the heavens like?*
3. *He said to them:*
4. *It is like a grain of mustard,*
5. *smaller than all seeds;*
6. *but when it falls on the tilled earth,*
7. *it sends forth a large stem*
8. *and becomes a shelter for the birds of the sky.*

96

1. *Jesus said:*
2. *The Kingdom of the Father is like a woman,*
3. *who took a little leaven,*
4. *hid it in dough*
5. *and of it made large loaves.*
6. *He who has ears let him hear!*

The final part of
Behold, the sower went out. (logion 9)
tells us that only a person who earnestly seeks the words of Jesus, who has the urge to open the heart to his presence within, will provide the good earth in which they will grow a hundred-fold.

The Way to the Kingdom

94
1. *Jesus said:*
2. *He who seeks shall find,*
3. *and to him who knocks it shall be opened.*

54
1. *Jesus said:*
2. *Happy are the poor,*
3. *for yours is the Kingdom of the heavens.*

6
1. *His disciples questioned, they said to him:*
2. *Do you wish that we should fast?*
3. *And in which way should we pray?*
4. *Should we give alms?*
5. *and what diet should we observe?*
6. *Jesus said:*

(6)
7 Do not lie,
8 and do not do what you dislike,
9 for all things are revealed before heaven.
10 For there is nothing hidden that shall not be manifest,
11 and there is nothing concealed
12 that shall remain without being revealed.

99
1 The disciples said to him:
2 Your brothers and your mother are standing outside.
3 He said to them:
4 Those here who do the wish of my Father
5 they are my brothers and my mother.
6 These are they
7 who shall enter the Kingdom of my Father.

12

1. The disciples said to Jesus:
2. We realize that you will go away from us;
3. who is it that will be great over us?
4. Jesus said to them:
5. Whatever place you have come to,
6. you will go to James the righteous,
7. because of whom heaven and earth came into being.

78

1. Jesus said:
2. Why did you come forth to the country?
3. To see a reed shaken by the wind
4/5. and to see a man clothed in soft garments?
6. See, your kings and your nobles;
7. these are clothed in soft garments,
8. and they will not be able to Know the Truth.

81

1. Jesus said:
2. He who has become spiritually rich,
3. let him become king;
4. and he who has temporal power,
5. let him renounce it!

57

1. Jesus said:
2. The Kingdom of the Father is like a man
3. who owned good seed.
4. His enemy came by night,
5. he sowed weeds among the good seed.
6. The man did not allow the labourers to pull up the weeds;
7. he said to them: lest perhaps you should go,
8. saying "we will pull up the weeds,"
9. and you pull up the wheat with it.
10. For on the day of the harvest
11. the weeds will appear;
12. they will be pulled up and will be burned.

64

1. Jesus said:
2. A man had guests
3. and when he had prepared the dinner
4. he sent his servant to invite the guests.
5. He went to the first
6. and said to him:
7. "My master invites you."
8. He said:
9. "I have some money for some traders;
10. they will come to me in the evening,
11. I will go and place orders with them.
12. I ask to be excused from the dinner."
13. He went to another
14. he said to him:
15. "My master invites you."
16. He said to him:
17. "I have bought a house and they request me for a day.
18. I will not be available."
19. He came to another
20. he said to him:
21. "My master invites you."
22. He said to him:

(64)

23 "My friend is to be married
24 and I am to arrange a feast;
25 I shall not be able to come.
26 I ask to be excused from the dinner."
27 He went to another
28 he said to him:
29 "My master invites you."
30 He said to him:
31 "I have bought a farm,
32 I go to collect the rent
33 I shall not be able to come,
34 I ask to be excused."
35 The servant came;
36 he said to his master:
37 "Those whom you have invited to the dinner have excused themselves."
38 The master said to his servant
39 "Go outside to the roads,
40 bring those whom you will find,
41 so that they may dine."
42 Those preoccupied with material concerns
43 shall not enter
44 the Place of my Father.

85

1. Jesus said:
2. Adam came into being from a great power
3. and a great richness,
4. and he was not worthy of you;
5. for had he been worthy,
6. he would not have tasted death.

110

1. Jesus said:
2. He who has found the world
3. and become rich,
4. let him deny the world!

Many people may be drawn to a Teaching on 'The Way' for which many sayings are included in the Thomas Text. When looked on as a whole, they are unusual in seeming to have a certain negativeness. On closer consideration however it may be seen that the negative tone applies to material or objective qualities. Thus it becomes clear that Jesus was working to dispel those—even though they so readily come to mind—because essentially they all belong to the realm of ahamkāra.

This is well shown in the long story of the feast

A man had guests (logion 64)

which in its outward form refers to preoccupation with worldly affairs. Yet inwardly it is also about the many excuses arising from ahamkāra that we all too easily find for not accepting 'the call' or, more dangerously, ignoring it.

Nevertheless discrimination needs to be applied. For if

Why did you come forth to the country (logion 78)

were to be regarded as a call to the life of an ascetic it would only be to see the first level of meaning. It is the final phrase that directs us towards non-attachment to worldly things.

In *We realize that you will go away from us* (logion 12)

this dialogue refers to James, one of the blood brothers of Jesus, who came in due course to take a leading part amongst the group of disciples of Jewish background—not yet a Church—that became established in Jerusalem. The final phrase is one that would have been familiar to his Jewish hearers.

Spiritual Richness

63

1. Jesus said:
2. There was a rich man
3. who had much wealth.
4. He said:
5. I will use my wealth
6. in order that I may sow and reap and plant,
7. and fill my storehouses with produce
8. so that I lack nothing.
9. This was what he thought in his heart;
10. and during that night he died.
11. He who has ears let him hear!

60

1. They saw a Samaritan,
2. carrying a lamb,
3. going into Judea.
4. He said to his disciples:
5. Why does this man carry the lamb around?
6. They said to him:
7. In order that he may kill it and eat it.
8. He said to them:
9. As long as it is alive
10. he will not eat it,
11. but only if he kills it
12. and it becomes a corpse.
13. They said:
14. Otherwise he will not be able to do it.
15. He said to them:
16. You yourselves, seek after a Place for yourselves
17. within Repose,
18. lest you become corpses
19. and be eaten.

90

1 Jesus said:
2 Come to me,
3 for easy is my yoke
4 and my lordship is gentle,
5 and you shall find repose for yourselves.

51

1 His disciples said to him:
2 On which day
3 will the repose of the dead come about?
4 And on which day
5 will the new world come?
6 He said to them:
7 What you expect has come
8 but you, you recognize it not.

113

1 *His disciples said to him:*
2 *On which day will the Kingdom come?*
3 *Jesus said: It will not come by expectation.*
4 *They will not say:*
5 *"Behold, it is here!"*
6 *or "Behold, there!"*
7 *But the Kingdom of the Father is spread out over the earth*
8 *and men do not see it.*

There was a rich man (logion 63)
is clearly a warning against the abuse of knowledge—filling the internal storehouses—and boasting of it. This could result in spiritual pride.

Come to me, for easy is my yoke (logion 90)
The meaning underlying the word yoke is a joining together. Here the joining to Jesus leads to a repose.

On which day will the repose of the dead come about?
(logion 51)
A cardinal feature of this Teaching is that the true Life can be found and known during this life, rather than being only in some life after death or in a messianic future or at the millenium.

Monakos and Courage

16
1. Jesus said:
2. Perhaps men think that I have come
3. to cast tranquility upon the earth;
4. they do not realize that perhaps my coming
5. will cast divisions upon the earth;
6. even fire, sword, strife!
7. For there may be five in a home,
8. three will be against two,
9. and two against three,
10. the father against the son,
11. and the son against the father;
12. then they shall stand boldly, being monakos.

49
1. Jesus said:
2. Happy are the monakos and the chosen
3. for you shall find the Kingdom.
4. Because you are from the heart of it,
5. you shall return there again.

75

1 *Jesus said:*
2/3 *There are many standing at the door,*
4 *but the monakos are they*
5 *who shall enter the marriage place.*

55

1 *Jesus said:*
2 *He who does not turn away from his father and his mother*
3 *will not be able to become my disciple,*
4 *and he who does not turn away from his brothers and sisters*
5 *and does not carry his cares in my way,*
6 *will not be worthy of me.*

   Three times in the Thomas Text Jesus employs the rarely used Greek word monakos. It does not translate into English. The nearest is the rather unsatisfactory word 'loner', in the sense of the nineteenth century American phrase "Go west, young man". In South Africa then they were called Pioneers, and were whole families. It implies foremost an independence, with perhaps something of an adventure about it. It means one who is willing to go forward on his own, who can become detached as a liner loosens its moorings to set out on a voyage.

MONAKOS AND COURAGE

In *Perhaps men think that I have come* (logion 16)
the Coptic word in phrase 5 carries a sense of a positive type of division, a discrimination. Then, to stand boldly as a monakos requires a certain sort of Courage; with a kind of determination and resolution. To walk one's spiritual life with independence, without going with the herd, whether that be in the community or within the family. It is because what Jesus came for was new, something different. That Courage resides in and comes from the Real Self.

In *Happy are the monakos and the chosen* (logion 49)
the word 'chosen' carries the sense of being separated rather than being favoured.

He who does not turn away from his father and mother
(logion 55)

To 'turn away from' is a rather free rendering of the Greek word miseo in phrases 2 and 5, which has no English equivalent to give its right flavour; it is a contrast with 'to love', for which we would need to invent a word 'to dis-love'.

However, here and in logion 101 (page 49), the inner meaning is 'to detach from', a separation of the psyche, as given more specifically in the following paraphrase:

*He who does not free himself from attachment to his father
and his mother
will not be able to become my disciple,
and he who does not free himself from his brothers and
sisters
and does not live every part of his life in my way,
will not be worthy of me.*

This word, and the Greek word monakos, and also the more recent term 'non-attachment', all point to the same concept. Specifically, in this saying, 'father, mother, brothers, sisters' may be applied to the religion of one's family upbringing.

Images

22

1. Jesus saw children who were being suckled.
2. He said to his disciples:
3. These children who are being suckled are like
4. those who enter the Kingdom.
5. They said to him:
6. Shall we then, being children,
7. enter the Kingdom?
8. Jesus said to them:
9. When you make the two One,
10. and you make the inner as the outer,
11. and the outer as the inner,
12. and the above as the below,
13. so that you will make the male and the female
14. into a single One,
15. in order that the male is not made male
16. nor the female made female;
17. when you make eyes in place of an eye,
18. and a hand in place of a hand,
19. and a foot in place of a foot,
20. and an image in place of an image,
21. then shall you enter the Kingdom.

50

1. *Jesus said:*
2. *If they say to you:*
3. *"Where are you from?"*
4. *say to them:*
5. *"We came from the Light*
6. *there, where the Light was,*
7. *by itself.*
8. *It stood boldly*
9. *and manifested itself in their image."*
10. *If they say to you:*
11. *"Who are you?"*
12/13. *say: "We are his sons*
14. *and we are the chosen of the Living Father."*
15. *If they question you:*
16. *"What is the sign of your Father in you?"*
17. *say to them:*
18. *"It is a movement with a repose."*

83

1. Jesus said:
2. The images are manifest to man
3. and the light that is amongst them is hidden.
4. In the image of the <u>L</u>ight of the Father
5. the <u>L</u>ight will reveal itself
6. and his image is hidden by his <u>L</u>ight.

84

1. Jesus said:
2. In the days you see your resemblance,
3. you rejoice.
4. But when you will see your images
5. that in the beginning were in you,
6. which neither die nor are manifest,
7. oh! how will you bear the revelation!

IMAGES

These are the four sayings whereby Jesus prompts us to explore his highly evolved concept of Images. There must have been some of his disciples, devotedly following him with their lives changed, who had not risen to the level of this concept. So it may be for some today; yet that may come with the passage of several years.

The word used in the Thomas Text is the Greek eikōn from which we get icon. An image may be thought of as being like a casting derived from a pattern; it is an exact replica, not the original nor is it a reproduction. An icon is not a representation. Michelangelo gave us on the ceiling of the Sistine Chapel the greatest visual representation of God, to convey symbolically by the touch of fingers the passing of divine quality into man. An icon of the Eastern Orthodox Church is different. It is an exact copy, but not the original, of a form invested with spiritual significance. The artist who paints each particular icon serves a long training under a master, and makes a copy that retains all the qualities of the original, thereby conveying the symbolism unsullied.

The wonderful saying
Jesus saw children being suckled (logion 22)
which we have already had occasion to consider, comprises a hierarchical series of phrases each one contrasting a spiritual form with a mental or material form. So when image occurs as the penultimate phrase it is telling us to find the spiritual meaning of 'icon'.

Note furthermore that image occurs as the last of the four phrases 17 to 20 where we are being invited to go with Jesus into a region that is beyond mental processes. It is a concept beyond the spiritual eye, beyond the physical hand or foot, up in a region of its own.

So in the first of these sayings we are being led to find a spiritual form of something that previously may have been a mental idea; to rise to the spiritual level above a mere thought-form. It is one of the gateways into the Kingdom.

IMAGES

In phrases 5 to 9 of:
If they say to you "Where are you from?" (logion 50)
the two sentences speak of our coming from the self-existing light; we saw this in the baby, and hence in ourselves. But in the third phrase we are suddenly taken to a very much higher level. The light was manifested in their image. 'Their' relates to 'we', these are the only plural words in the saying. So, however startling it may seem, we are being told the light is the image of us. The original is the highest in mankind, the light is its replica.

The images are manifest to man (logion 83)
starts with the mental images we make but, because they come from ahamkāra—of which the ordinary mind is a part—the light within them is hidden. However, the Light of the Father is the true Light and, as we find that, the true Light reveals itself. So far, so good. However, we need to look at the third phrase more closely. It is not saying the image of the Father, such as in the idea we might have of 'man being made in the image of God'. It is the first part of a longer expression that spans over three phrases. In the last of those 'his image is hidden' is a way of saying the Father is imageless, he is the original. And so his imageless nature is hidden by his Light. This is the same as where we can say 'the light reveals', and 'the brilliance of the light conceals'. Yet we have also been told that the Light is the image of man. So this is a paradox of the conjunction of opposites, for the grasping of which it is necessary to get beyond the words and the mind—to get into the experience of Oneness which usually can only be found in contemplation. Here we have an instance of a description of the indescribable, a definition of the indefinable, an expression of the inexpressible. This is a *via media* attempting to convey something that cannot be expressed in language, but only experienced.

The days you see your resemblance, (logion 84)
This saying is a complement to the preceding one. In its first phrase it reminds us of the rejoicing we feel as we recognize that

what is at our Centre resembles the Light. Then, going on, we come to see that this image was pre-existent, it does not need to manifest itself because it was always there, and it is not affected by our death. Put another way, the image of the Light within us is eternal, not in the sense that it goes on for ever but in the much more profound sense that it is independent of time. It is just in this way that by finding the inner meaning of these sayings one will find Life that is independent of death. This, indeed, can be a revelation that is almost overwhelming.

Happiness

68
1. *Jesus said:*
2. *Happy are you*
3. *when you are disliked*
4. *and you are pursued;*
5. *and no Place will be found there,*
6. *where you have been pursued in the heart.*

69
1. *Jesus said:*
2. *Happy are they*
3. *who have been pursued in their heart.*
4. *It is they*
5. *who have Known the Father in Truth.*
6. *Happy are they who are hungry,*
7. *so that the belly of those who desire*
   to see Truth shall be satisfied.

54

1. Jesus said:
2. Happy are the poor,
3. for yours is the Kingdom of the heavens.

58

1. Jesus said:
2. Happy is the man who has toiled to lose ahamkāra,
3. he has found the Life.

103

1. Jesus said:
2. Happy is the man who knows
3. where and when the robbers will creep in;
4. so that he will arise
5. and gather his strength
6. and prepare for action
7. before they come.

HAPPINESS

7

1 Jesus said:
2 Happy is the lion which the man will eat,
3 and the lion will become man;
4 and abominated is the man whom the lion will eat,
5 and the lion will become man.

18

1 The disciples said to Jesus:
2 Tell us in what way our end will be.
3 Jesus said:
4 Have you therefore discerned the beginning
5 since you seek after the end?
6 For in the Place where the beginning is,
7 there will be the end.
8 Happy is he who will stand boldly at the beginning,
9 he shall Know the end,
10 and shall find Life independent of death.

19
1. Jesus said:
2/3. Happy is he who already was before he is.
4. If you become my disciples
5. and hear my logia,
6. even these stones will minister to you.
7. For you have five trees in Paradise
8. which are unchanged in summer or winter
9. and their leaves do not fall away.
10. He who knows them
11. shall find life independent of death.

49
1. Jesus said:
2. Happy are the monakos and the chosen
3. for you shall find the Kingdom.
4. Because you are from the heart of it,
5. you shall return there again.

90

1. Jesus said:
2. Come to me,
3. for easy is my yoke
4. and my lordship is gentle,
5. and you shall find repose for yourselves.

HAPPINESS

The ten sayings in which Jesus refers to Happiness have been grouped together to emphasise that this is one of the themes he spoke of most frequently, using the Greek word makarios. The only key-words used more frequently in the Thomas Text are the Kingdom, to find, to Know, the living and the Light.

It is apparent that the sayings of Jesus with makarios must have been given on many different occasions, as prompted by the opportunity or situation. Can we allow ourselves to visualize Jesus going about with his disciples—which the chauvinistic assumptions of the evangelists limited to the twelve with hardly any mention of the women who must have also been present—carrying an aura about him that led to the frequent use of this word?

Even so, happiness and to be happy in English may not immediately carry the intended meaning. It is not so much merriment as joy or bliss, associated with a profound contentment that leads to a repose. It does not appear so much as laughter (although it may come as a great challenge to us to visualize Jesus laughing with his disciples) but as a poise and radiance. It is derived not from a response to external events but from a condition or state of being within. It may be regarded as a flowering of the Self, so that any of the sayings 'Happy is he who does so-and-so' is a pointer towards coming to an awareness of what lies within.

Thus this emphasis, both here and in the sayings of Jesus, stems directly from Happiness being one of the facets of the jewel that comprises spiritual Truth.

Old Order and New Way

34

1 Jesus said:
2 If a blind man guides the Being of a blind man,
3 both of them fall to the bottom of the pit.

46

1 Jesus said:
2 From Adam until John the Baptist,
3 among the children begotten of women
4 there is none higher than John the Baptist,
5 such that his vision will be able to see Truth.
6 But I have said:
7 He who amongst you becomes as a child
8 shall Know the Kingdom,
9 and he shall be higher than John.

OLD ORDER AND NEW WAY

52
1. *His disciples said to him:*
2. *Twenty-four prophets spoke in Israel*
3. *and they all spoke about your nature.*
4. *He said to them:*
5. *You have ignored Him who is living before you*
6. *and you have spoken about the dead.*

39
1. *Jesus said:*
2. *The Pharisees and the scribes*
3. *took the keys of Knowledge,*
4. *and they hid them.*
5. *Neither did they enter,*
6. *nor did they allow*
7. *those who wished to enter.*
8. *But you, become prudent as serpents*
9. *and innocent even as doves.*

102

1 Jesus said:
2 Woe to them, the Pharisees!
3 For they resemble a dog
4 sleeping in the oxen's manger;
5 for neither does he eat
6 nor does he allow the oxen to eat.

43

1 His disciples said to him:
2 Who are you that you should say these things to us?
3 [Jesus said to them:] From what I say to you
4 are you not aware who I am?
5 But you, you were even as the Jews:
6 for they love the tree,
7 they dislike its fruit;
8 and they love the fruit,
9 they dislike the tree.

53

1. *His disciples said to him:*
2. *Is circumcision beneficial or not?*
3. *He said to them:*
4. *If it were beneficial,*
5. *their father would beget them circumcised from their mother.*
6. *But the loss of ahamkāra*
7. *gives the ultimate benefit.*

47

1 Jesus said:
2 It is impossible
3 for a man to mount two horses,
4 for him to stretch two bows;
5 and it is impossible
6 for a servant to serve two masters,
7 otherwise he will honour the one
8 and offend the other.
9 Let a man drink old wine
10 and now he wants to drink new wine.
11 And new wine is not poured
12 into old wineskins,
13 lest they should burst;
14 and old wine is not poured
15 into a new wineskin,
16 lest this be spoiled.
17 An old patch is not sewn
18 on to a new garment,
19 because there would be a division.

Something new is an emphatic theme of the Thomas Text. That is to say, in these sayings of Jesus he was asserting that what he was presenting was new. It was not just an advance, development or progression of what was before, but was a new departure for those who heard and saw him inwardly.

Twenty-four prophets spoke in Israel (logion 52)

Jesus contrasts the views of the disciples, that the revelations of the Prophets are what is significant, with the living word he is giving them.

It is impossible for a man to mount two horses (logion 47)

is the most telling on this theme, if only because of the impact of the reiteration of very simple everyday situations familiar to people who came chiefly from the countryside. Seven word-pictures are given as a coherent series, all emphasising the same point and building up the impact.

In those days old wine, stored in wineskins, was stale wine. The division, as the word is used here, of a garment could be called a rent.

The gospels of the Bible tell of two occasions when he spoke to the four- or the five-thousand. What he gave them was sustenance, so 'all were satisfied'. Perhaps inaudible to some of them, they could see him with both their outer eyes and their inner eye. With that, they saw something new, and it was satisfying.

We cannot see him with our outer eyes. But let them dwell on a copy, the best that can be obtained, of his radiant living form portrayed in an icon of the Eastern Orthodox Church. Let this be put in some special place of your home. Let living flowers be always kept beside it. Spend some minutes of every day before it, gazing intently. Then the inner eye may come to see him. There will be something new, and it too will be satisfying.

Beyond Feminity

114

1 Simon Peter said to them:
2 Let Mary go out from amongst us,
3 because women are not worthy of the Life.
4 Jesus said:
5 Behold, I will guide her Being,
6 in order that I make her male
7/8 that she, like you, shall become a living spirit.
9 For every person who transcends being woman or man
10 shall enter the Kingdom of the heavens.

BEYOND FEMINITY

22

1. *Jesus saw children who were being suckled.*
2. *He said to his disciples:*
3. *These children who are being suckled are like*
4. *those who enter the Kingdom.*
5. *They said to him:*
6. *Shall we then, being children,*
7. *enter the Kingdom?*
8. *Jesus said to them:*
9. *When you make the two One,*
10. *and you make the inner as the outer,*
11. *and the outer as the inner,*
12. *and the above as the below,*
13. *so that you will make the male and the female*
14. *into a single One,*
15. *in order that the male is not made male*
16. *nor the female made female;*
17. *when you make eyes in place of an eye,*
18. *and a hand in place of a hand,*
19. *and a foot in place of a foot,*
20. *and an image in place of an image,*
21. *then shall you enter the Kingdom.*

101

1. *He who does not turn away from his father and his mother*
2. *in my way*
3. *will not be able to become my disciple;*
4. *and he who does not love his Father and his Mother*
5. *in my way*
6. *will not be able to become my disciple;*
7. *for my mother has begotten me*
8. *but my true Mother gave me life.*

105

1. *Jesus said:*
2. *He who knows the Father and the Mother,*
3. *will be beyond all worldly parentage.*

Masculinity and femininity are a duality. Jesus urges us to go beyond that, to rise to something higher. His aim is to teach us to experience Oneness.

Wealth in Poverty

29
1. *Jesus said:*
2. *If the flesh has come into being because of the spirit,*
3. *it is a marvel;*
4. *but if the spirit has come into being because of the body,*
5. *it is a marvel of marvels.*
6. *But I, I marvel at this:*
7. *about this great richness of spiritual Truth*
8. *put within this poor world of objects.*

Austerity

27
1 If you transcend not the world of objects,
2 you will not find the Kingdom;
3 if you keep not the sabbath as a true sabbath,
4 you will not behold the Father.

56
1 Jesus said:
2 He who has known the world,
3 has found a corpse;
4 and he who has found a corpse
5 of him the world is not worthy.

80
1 Jesus said:
2 He who has known the world
3 has found the body;
4 but he who has found the body
5 of him the world is not worthy.

AUSTERITY

It is easy to imagine that as Jesus walked about his country, staying where he could, he lived a life of some austerity. At least the evidence is that he turned his back on luxury and all intemperance. Thomas, accompanying him, would have shared this.

Certainly these sayings are compatible with those of other spiritual Teachers, as they urge their followers to forego those indulgences that are attractive to the body and the physical senses—it is an essential preliminary in the training of every Tibetan Buddhist monk. Those only serve to feed ahamkāra.

On the other hand, discrimination is needed to distinguish between such cleansing of one's material life and any abnegation or asceticism. That would merely lead back to the realm of ahamkāra in a negative sense.

It is not possible to tell why Thomas repeated two of these sayings, differing only in a single Greek word ptōma a corpse and sōma a body—no other saying is repeated. They occur quite widely separated in the original Thomas Text, and the most simple explanation is that while dictating to the scribe he merely forgot that he had recorded the saying once already.

Jesus' Disappointment

31
1. Jesus said:
2. No prophet is accepted in his own village;
3. no physician heals those who recognize him.

74
1. He said:
2. Lord, there are many around the well
3. but none in the well.

73
1. Jesus said:
2. The harvest is indeed great,
3. but the labourers are few.
4. Entreat, therefore, the Lord
5. to send labourers to the harvest.

JESUS' DISAPPOINTMENT

92

1 Jesus said:
2 Seek and you will find.
3 But those things
4 that you asked me in those days
5 I did not tell you then;
6 now I desire to tell them
7 but you do not seek after them.

91

1 They said to him:
2 Tell us who you are
3 so that we may believe in you.
4 He said to them:
5 You scrutinize the face of heaven and earth,
6 and him who is before you
7 you have not known,
8 and you know not how to probe this
                                            revelation.

38

1 *Jesus said:*
2 *Many times have you longed to hear these logia*
3 *which I say to you,*
4 *and you have no other*
5 *from whom to hear them.*
6 *There will be days*
7 *when you seek after me*
8 *and you will not find me.*

86

1 *Jesus said:*
2 *The foxes have their dens*
3 *and the birds have their nest,*
4 *but the Son of man has no place*
5 *to lay his head and to rest.*

JESUS' DISAPPOINTMENT

65

1 He said:
2 A benevolent man had a vineyard.
3 He gave it to husbandmen
4 so that they would work it
5 and he would receive his produce from their
6 He sent his servant   hands.
7 in order that the husbandmen would give him
8 the fruit of the vineyard
9 They laid hold of his servant,
10 they beat him;
11 a little more and they would have killed him.
12/13 The servant went, he reported to his master.
14 His master said:
15 "Perhaps he did not know them."
16 He sent another servant;
17 the husbandmen beat him also.
18 Then the owner sent his son;
19 he said:
20 "Perhaps they will respect my son."
21 Because those husbandmen realized
22 that he was the heir to the vineyard,
23 they seized him, they killed him.
24 He who has ears let him hear!

66

1 *Jesus said:*
2 *Show me the stone*
3 *which the builders have rejected:*
4 *it is that, the corner-stone.*

There are an appreciable number of sayings in which the disciples or other listeners had come with pre-suppositions or had failed to understand Jesus, and he works to correct their awareness. There are a few in which he can only challenge them to rise to something better. But in:

A benevolent man had a vineyard (logion 65)
and *Show me the stone* (logion 66)

he seems almost to have despaired of some of his people—parables of rejection and even killing. Nevertheless, it does seem necessary to draw the surprising and disconcerting conclusion that Jesus felt disappointment that his Teachings were not being recognized or accepted.

Wise Sayings

25

1. Jesus said:
2. Love your brother even as your own soul,
3. guard him
4. even as the pupil of your eye.

26

1. Jesus said:
2. The mote that is in your brother's eye
3. you see,
4. but the beam that is in your own eye
5. you see not.
6. When you cast the beam out of your eye,
7. then you will see clearly
8. to cast the mote out of your brother's eye.

32

1 Jesus said:
2 A city built on a high mountain
3 and made strong
4 cannot fall,
5 nor can it be hidden.

34

1 Jesus said:
2 If a blind man guides the Being of a blind man,
3 both of them fall to the bottom of the pit.

23

1 Jesus said:
2 I will choose you, one out of ten thousand,
3 and two out of ten thousand,
4 and they shall stand boldly being a single One.

WISE SAYINGS

95

1 *Jesus said:*
2 *If you have money,*
3 *do not lend at interest,*
4 *but give it*
5 *to him who will not return it.*

93

1 *Give not what is pure to dogs,*
2 *lest they cast it on the dung-heap.*
3 *Throw not pearls to swine*
4 *lest they pollute them.*

The Consummation

2
Jesus said:
1. Let him who seeks not cease from seeking
2. until he finds;
3. and when he finds,
4. he will be turned around,
5. and when he is turned around
6. he will marvel
7. and he shall reign over the All.

3

1. *Jesus said:*
2. *If those who guide your Being say to you:*
3. *"Behold the Kingdom is in the heaven,"*
4. *then the birds of the sky will precede you;*
5. *if they say to you: "It is in the sea,"*
6. *then the fish will precede you.*
7. *But the Kingdom is in your centre*
8. *and is about you.*
9. *When you Know your Selves*
10. *then you will be Known,*
11. *and you will be aware that you are*
12. *the sons of the Living Father.*
13. *But if you do not Know yourselves*
14. *then you are in poverty,*
15. *and you are the poverty.*

THE CONSUMMATION

It will now be possible to find the full inner meanings hidden in the sayings of the summary of the Teachings which Thomas —in oriental fashion—wrote at the start of his Text.

Seek is the word it starts with, just as seeking is the start of the spiritual journey. Yet the precursor for that is a sincere and ardent urge to seek, to be pursued in the heart by that urge.

One who does not cease from such seeking shall find. It is a promise given repeatedly by Jesus that has no conditions, it is unqualified. It involves only him and the individual, there is no intermediary.

However, he warns, the seeker on finding will be turned around. This may be no more than a pool of clear water in a mountain stream being stirred. More often it involves leaving behind old luggage from previous teachings. It may mean becoming detached from father and mother in his way, of having the Courage to go out as a monakos. It most probably means the quenching of ahamkāra—which may come gradually like flour trickling from a broken jar, or may involve the strength and resolution of killing a giant; it may even mean going through a fire.

But such turning around gives rise to marvelling. The wonder of being emptied of ahamkāra results in a peace, tranquillity and repose that goes beyond the power of mere words to express.

Jesus can gently lampoon the other guides from the old way. And he can warn that those who have not come to Know their Real Selves not only live in poverty, in the darkness of spiritual blindness, in a bondage to ahamkāra, but they are the poverty. Not just impoverished but—the ancient Coptic is quite clear about it—that poverty itself.

However, he says—speaking to his Jewish listeners—the Kingdom is at one's centre and it is all about one. The access to that Kingdom is to Know—in its deepest meaning—the Real Self. Furthermore, this is a reciprocal knowing, between the individual and the Father. Those comprise a duality, yet as they merge they become Known as a Oneness.

THE CONSUMMATION

Then, speaking to his hearers using the Greek idiom, he refers to that Oneness as the All, which in our modern idiom is the Ultimate or Ultimate Reality. Taking these two ways of speaking together, he who finds, is troubled and marvels, reigns over the All, becomes the King of the Kingdom. It is the ultimate mystical experience of Oneness whereby, assimilating his words, the individual becomes as him, and he becomes as the individual. At that Ultimate there can be nothing further, just tranquil joy and happiness exists.

Acknowledgements

The following source-books were of especial value for making the translation of the Thomas Text that forms the basis of this Presentation. They are all rare. Only a few are in print, and several of them are not even likely to be found in libraries.

'The Gospel According to Thomas' by A Guillaumont, H-Ch Puech, G Quispel, W Till and Yassah 'Abd Al Masīḥ. Published 1959 and 1976 by E Brill, Leyden, Holland. Professor Quispel first identified the Thomas Text and brought photographs of it to the West. These scholars were the first to make good the small defects, and translate it into a European language. They identified the individual sayings, and gave the numbers to them.

'L'Évangile Selon Thomas' by Phillipe de Suarez. Published 1975 by Association Métanoïa, 26200, Montélimar, France. This has the unique value of providing a concordance, in French, Coptic and Greek, of all the words used in the Thomas Text; it also gives cross-references to entries in the great dictionaries. The present author has made his own concordance, in card-index form, in English, Coptic and Greek, of the words used in this present translation.

'Évangile Selon Thomas' by É Gillabert, P Bourgeois and Y Haas. Published 1979 by Association Métanoïa. Although with the same title and publishers as the foregoing, and using the same translation of the Thomas Text into French, this is entirely different. It is noteworthy in giving many of the inner meanings of the sayings, and these notes are written in very erudite French. The 1979 version has the unique and very special value of giving a word-by-word interlinear translation from the Coptic into French. Inexplicably the 1994 reprint omits that. The Association Métanoïa scholars identified the short Semitic phrases, and gave them phrase-numbers. Also the Bible references given here on pages 28 and 29 were established by them.

'The Nag Hammadi Library in English' edited by J M Robinson, translations of the Coptic texts by T O Lambdin. Published 1977 by E J Brill. The definitive treatment of all the other books found at Nag Hammâdi.

'A Coptic Dictionary' by W E Crum. Published 1962 by Oxford University Press. Coptic, English and Greek. A majestic lifetime's work by an Oxford don. The present author has made a sub-set of this with only the Coptic words used in the Thomas Text.

'An Introductory Coptic Grammar (Sahidic Dialect)' by J M Plumley. Published 1948 by Home & van Thal, London. Rather than being set in type, the whole of this is photo-reproduced from a hand-written manuscript.

'An Elementary Coptic Grammar of the Sahidic Dialect' by C C Walters. Published 1983 by Blackwell, Oxford, England. This is photo-reproduced from a typescript.

'A Greek-English Lexicon of the New Testament and Other Early Christian Literature' translated and adapted by W F Arndt and F W Gingrich from the German work by Walter Bauer. Published 1957 by University of Chicago Press, USA. The present author has made a sub-set of only the Greek words used in the Thomas Text.

Index to Sayings

This index gives the page references of all the sayings in the order they appear in the original Thomas Text.

0	These are the hidden logia	page 33
1	He who finds the inner meaning of these logia	33
2	Let him who seeks not cease from seeking	33 & 143
3	If those who guide your Being say to you:	34 & 51 & 144
4	The man old in days will not hesitate	79
5	Know Him who is before your face,	41 & 52
6	His disciples questioned, they said to him:	96
7	Happy is the lion which the man will eat,	72 & 119
8	The man is like a wise fisherman	37 & 79
9	Behold, the sower went out.	94
10	I have cast fire upon the world,	63 & 71
11	This heaven will pass away,	82
12	We realize that you will go away from us;	98
13	Make a comparison to me	45
14	If you fast you will beget a sin to yourselves,	39
15	When you behold Him who was not begotten of woman,	42
16	Perhaps men think that I have come to cast tranquility upon the earth;	108
17	I will give you what no eye has seen,	41
18	Tell us in what way our end will be.	57 & 119
19	Happy is he who already was before he is.	58 & 120
20	Tells us, what is the Kingdom of the heavens like?	95
21	Mary said to Jesus: whom do your disciples resemble?	68
22	Jesus saw children who were being suckled.	81 & 111 & 130
23	I will choose you, one out of a thousand,	84 & 141

INDEX TO SAYINGS

24	*Show us the Place where you are,*	60
25	*Love your brother even as your own soul,*	140
26	*The mote that is in your brother's eye*	140
27	*If you abstain not from the world,*	133
28	*I stood boldly in the midst of the world*	55 & 71
29	*If the flesh has come into being because of the spirit,*	132
30	*The place where there are three gods*	84
31	*No prophet is accepted in his own village;*	135
32	*A city built on a high mountain*	141
33	*What you will hear in one ear*	60
34	*If a blind man guides the being of a blind man*	123 & 141
35	*It is not possible to enter the house of the strong man*	67
36	*Have no care, from morning to evening*	39
37	*On which day will you be manifest to us*	65
38	*Many times have you longed to hear these logia*	137
39	*The Pharisees and the scribes took the keys of knowledge*	124
40	*A vine was planted without the Father*	92
41	*He who has in his hand,*	92
42	*Become your Real Self, as ahamkāra passes away.*	72
43	*Who are you that you should say these things to us?*	125
44	*He who blasphemes against the Father,*	93
45	*Grapes are not harvested from thorn trees*	93
46	*From Adam until John the Baptist,*	52 & 123
47	*It is impossible for a man to mount two horses,*	127
48	*If two make peace with each other*	80
49	*Happy are the monakos and the chosen*	108 & 120
50	*If they say to you: "Where are you from?"*	61 & 112
51	*On which day will the repose of the dead come about?*	106
52	*Twenty-four prophets spoke in Israel*	124
53	*Is circumcision beneficial or not?*	126
54	*Happy are the poor,*	96 & 118
55	*He who does not turn away from his father and his mother*	109
56	*He who has known the world*	133
57	*The Kingdom of the Father is like a man*	99

INDEX TO SAYINGS

58	*Happy is the man who has toiled to lose ahamkāra*	64 & 118
59	*Look upon Him who is living*	42
60	*They saw a Samaritan, carrying a lamb,*	105
61	*Two will rest there on a couch:*	70
62	*I tell my mysteries to those who are worthy of my mysteries*	86
63	*There was a rich man who had much wealth.*	104
64	*A man had guests and when he had prepared the dinner*	100
65	*A benevolent man had a vineyard.*	138
66	*Show me the stone which the builders have rejected*	139
67	*He who understands the All,*	86
68	*Happy are you when you are disliked*	117
69	*Happy are they who have been pursued in their heart*	53 & 117
70	*When you bring forth that in yourselves,*	65
71	*I will overturn this house,*	64
72	*Tell my brothers to divide my father's possessions with me.*	85
73	*The harvest is indeed great,*	135
74	*Lord, there are many standing around the well*	135
75	*There are many standing at the door,*	109
76	*The Kingdom of the Father is like a man, a merchant,*	38 & 85
77	*I am the light that is above them all.*	44 & 87
78	*Why did you come forth to the country?*	53 & 98
79	*A woman from the multitude said to him:*	43
80	*He who has known the world*	133
81	*He who has become rich,*	99
82	*He who is near to me is near to the fire,*	43
83	*The images are manifest to man*	113
84	*In the days when you see your resemblance*	113
85	*Adam came into being from a great power*	102
86	*The foxes have their dens*	137
87	*Wretched is the body that depends on a body.*	83
88	*The angels with the prophets will come to you*	83
89	*Why do you wash the outside of the cup?*	40 & 84
90	*Come to me, for easy is my yoke*	106 & 121

INDEX TO SAYINGS

91	Tell us who you are so that we may believe in you.	54 & 136
92	Seek and you shall find.	136
93	Give not what is pure to dogs,	142
94	He who seeks shall find,	96
95	If you have money, do not lend at interest,	142
96	The Kingdom of the Father is like a woman, who took a little leaven,	95
97	The Kingdom of the Father is like a woman who was carrying a jar full of flour	66
98	The Kingdom of the Father is like a man wishing to kill a giant.	66
99	Your brothers and your mother are standing outside.	97
100	They showed Jesus a gold coin	50
101	He who does not turn away from his father and his mother	49 & 131
102	Woe to them, the Pharisees!	125
103	Happy is the man who knows	67 & 118
104	Come and let us pray and let us fast!	49
105	He who knows the Father and the Mother	54 & 131
106	When you make the two One,	80
107	The Kingdom is like a shepherd	37
108	He who drinks from my mouth	44
109	The Kingdom is like a man who owned in his field a hidden treasure,	62
110	He who has found the world	102
111	The heavens and the earth will roll back before you,	63
112	Woe to the flesh that depends upon the soul!	83
113	On which day will the Kingdom come?	107
114	Simon Peter said to them: Let Mary go out from amongst us,	129